insight text guide

Timothy Nolan

The Complete Maus

Art Spiegelman

First published in 2013, reprinted 2014 (twice), 2015, 2016, 2018, 2019, 2020, 2021, 2022, 2023 (twice), 2024, 2025.

Insight Publications Pty Ltd
3/350 Charman Road
Cheltenham VIC 3192
Australia
Tel: +61 3 8571 4950
Email: books@insightpublications.com.au

www.insightpublications.com.au

National Library of Australia Cataloguing-in-Publication entry:
Nolan, Timothy, author.
Spiegelman's The complete maus / Timothy Nolan.
9781922243140 (paperback)
Insight text guide.
Includes bibliographical references.
For secondary school age.
Spiegelman, Art. Maus
Spiegelman, Art—Criticism and interpretation.
741.5973

Other ISBNs:
9781925175189 (digital)

Cover design: The Modern Art Production Group

Printed by Markono Print Media Pte Ltd

contents

CHARACTER MAP

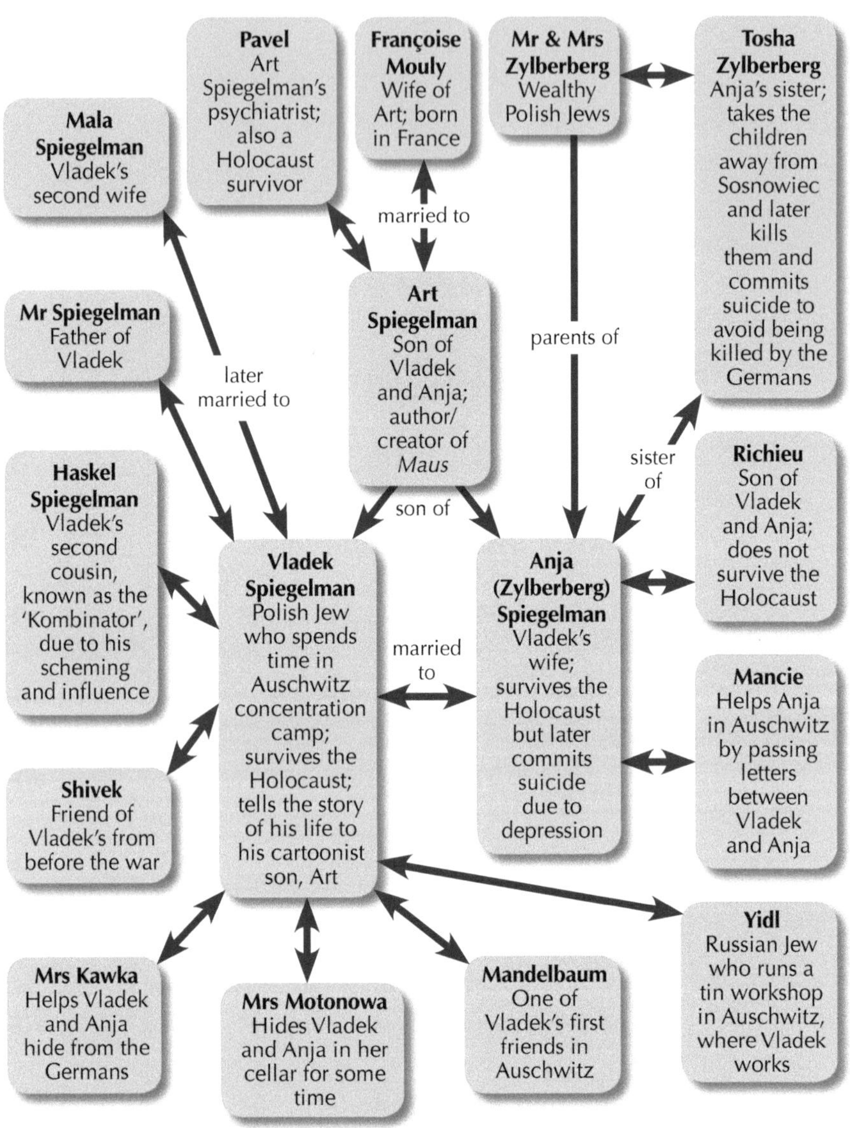

OVERVIEW

About the author

Art Spiegelman was born Itzhak Avraham ben Zeev on 15 February 1948 in Stockholm, Sweden. His parents, Vladek and Anja (nee Zylberberg) Spiegelman, were both survivors of the Jewish Holocaust of World War II (1939–1945). In 1951, when Art was three years old, the family moved to the United States.

Resisting his parents' aspirations for him to become a dentist, Spiegelman started drawing cartoons at the age of twelve by imitating the style of *Mad Magazine*. As a teenager he was offered work with United Features Syndicate, a commercial comic-strip service, but he turned it down as he believed in art primarily as expression and not as a money-making enterprise. While studying art and philosophy at university, Spiegelman played a prominent role in the underground 'comix subculture' of the 1960s and 1970s. He gained a reputation for being a philosophical and thoughtful artist, who advocated passionately and fervently for cartooning to be regarded as a serious art form. In his work, Spiegelman demonstrated that the graphic form could tell complex and dark stories just as effectively as the light-hearted and heroic stories for which comics had traditionally been known.

Spiegelman has spent much of his professional life providing opportunities for budding cartoonists to publish work and explore the medium. Together with his wife, notable artist and designer Françoise Mouly, Spiegelman founded *RAW*, a highly praised and celebrated avant-garde comics magazine, in 1980. He has also had a range of jobs in the comics industry. Between 1965 and 1987, Spiegelman was the creative consultant for Topps, an American manufacturer of chewing gum, candy and collectibles, best known for producing baseball cards. Between 1979 and 1986 he taught at the School of

Visual Arts in New York. And between 1993 and 2003, he was a staff artist and writer for *The New Yorker*, where he became lauded as one of the periodical's most sensational artists.

Today, Spiegelman lives in New York City with his wife, with whom he has two children. He has won many awards and is regarded as a highly significant artist and writer. In 2006 he was named one of *Time*'s 100 Most Influential People, and in 2011 he was awarded the Grand Prix at the Angoulême International Comics Festival. Spiegelman and Mouly have co-edited three comic anthologies for children, called *Big Fat Little Lit,* and publish a series of children's books presented in comic-book format, called *Toon Books*.

In order to differentiate between Art Spiegelman, the artist/author of *Maus*, and Artie, the character representation of Art Spiegelman in *Maus*, we will refer to the author as Spiegelman, and the character in the novel as Artie.

Synopsis

The story begins with a prologue, in which a boy, Artie, falls over while playing with friends. His father, Vladek, dismisses Artie's distress, saying, 'Friends? If you lock them together in a room with no food for a week … THEN you could see what it is, friends!' (p.6, frame 5).

Part One begins in 1938. Vladek is a Polish Jewish man living in Częstochowa, a city in southern Poland. He works in the textile industry, making enough for a comfortable life. Vladek begins a relationship with a local woman called Lucia, who proposes to him. He refuses, and soon marries Anja Zylberberg, a Jewish woman from a wealthy family. Together, they live in the town of Sosnowiec. Vladek buys a textile factory in Bielsko with the financial assistance of Anja's father. Soon after, Anja and Vladek have a son named Richieu, and Anja falls into postnatal depression, resulting in her spending three months in a sanatorium.

The following year, 1939, the war begins and Vladek is drafted to fight against Germany. He is at the front for mere hours before he is captured and becomes a prisoner of war. Vladek is sent to a camp where he is made to work in cold and gruelling conditions. He is released under the pretence that he and his fellow prisoners will be returned home to Sosnowiec. Instead, Vladek gets taken to Lublin, in the German-occupied section of Poland, where he is placed in another prisoner-of-war camp. He manages to bribe the Germans to release him to a friend of his uncle, Orbach. With Orbach's assistance, Vladek poses as a non-Jewish Pole in order to get back across the border to Sosnowiec.

Once home, Vladek returns to his normal life with his family for a couple of years. Yet the persecution of Jews slowly increases throughout Poland, with stories circulating of Jews going missing, 'never seen again' (p.77, frame 5). Strict curfews are put in place for the remaining Jews. Fear increases in Sosnowiec, as Germans close off streets and take large numbers of Jews away. Things get 'a little worse, a little worse' (p.81, frame 1) day by day, with the Germans, or 'Aryan managers' (p.78, frame 3), taking over Polish businesses and repossessing property simply because they can. Riots begin in the streets, and the Germans arrest, beat and deport Jews (presumably to the concentration camps) for no apparent reason.

In January 1942, all Jews in Sosnowiec are relocated to another German-occupied quarter of Poland, Stara Sosnowiec. This is a ghetto town, where Vladek and his family are made to live in much smaller dwellings. Jews are arrested and beaten for any supposed transgression, and hanged for dealing goods without coupons. One day, Jews are made to gather in their hundreds to be divided between those who will be sent away and those permitted to remain. It is here that the stories of Auschwitz begin to circulate among the Polish Jews.

In Stara Sosnowiec, Vladek and his family hide Anja's grandparents in a bunker to prevent them being deported to Auschwitz. Eventually, under pressure from the Germans, the family hand over Anja's grandparents and the remaining Jews of Sosnowiec are moved to a ghetto in Srodula. Vladek and Anja decide to send their son, Richieu, to live with Anja's sister, Tosha, in Zawiercie, an area they think is safe from the Germans. We learn that some months after Richieu is sent to Zawiercie, the Germans arrive there and begin to take Jews away; Tosha poisons herself and the children in order to save them from Auschwitz.

In Srodula the family hide as more and more people are deported; when they are found they are placed in a 'ghetto inside the ghetto' (p.115, frame 6), where Vladek meets his cousin Haskel, a chief of the Jewish police, and Haskel's brother, Miloch. Haskel cannot prevent Anja's parents from being sent to Auschwitz, but Miloch gets Vladek a job in a shoe factory, mending the boots of German soldiers. Miloch also shows Vladek a secret bunker that he has constructed in the hope of avoiding the inevitable deportation. They wait in this bunker until the ghetto is cleared and the Germans are gone. Then Anja and Vladek flee in the direction of Sosnowiec.

For the next few weeks Vladek and Anja struggle to hide in Sosnowiec. It is difficult to gain assistance from fellow Poles, as many non-Jews are unwilling to risk their lives to habour Jews. Eventually, Vladek and Anja meet Mrs Motonowa, who hides them in her cellar. Hoping to flee Sosnowiec, Vladek strikes a deal with people smugglers who assure him that they will smuggle him and Anja to Hungary. Once on the train to Hungary, the smugglers disappear and the Germans arrive. They arrest Vladek and Anja, who are taken to Auschwitz.

Upon their arrival, Vladek and Anja are separated, with Vladek going to the men's camp at Auschwitz I and Anja going to Auschwitz II-Birkenau. All prisoners are issued with uniforms and wooden shoes, and a number is tattooed on their left forearm, marking them as prisoners of war. Vladek soon realises that survival in Auschwitz is a test of wits and cunning, as well as a matter of luck, and his time in the camp leads him to one scheme and deal after another. He manages to befriend a Polish guard, a Kapo (a prisoner assigned to monitor other prisoners) who wants to learn English. The Kapo treats Vladek well, protecting him from the gas chambers. Vladek manages to secure a job mending the boots of German soldiers. He soon hears that new barracks are being constructed in Auschwitz I, and collects as many supplies as he can to bribe soldiers to bring Anja to these barracks so he can see her.

Vladek gets a job as a tinsmith, working for a surly man called Yidl. It is through this that Vladek becomes 'eyewitness' (p.229, frame 9) to the crematorium buildings in Auschwitz I. He describes, in great detail, the setup of these buildings, and recalls that those who worked in them told him that the Jews were gassed, and their bodies disposed of in the industrial ovens. Other Jews were thrown in giant pits – dead or alive – then doused with gasoline and burnt.

Gradually, the Allied Front draws nearer to the camp. Worried about impending conflict, the Germans force everyone on a death march, a 145-kilometre trek from Auschwitz to Breslau, Germany, the site of a smaller concentration camp. Malnourished and exhausted, many die. Prisoners are then marched out of this smaller camp and locked in a cattle train. They travel for days until they reach barracks in Dachau, Germany. Here Vladek contracts an infection and then typhus, a fever carried by lice that bite the skin. He comes close to death.

Eventually, the prisoners are taken to the Swiss border to be exchanged as prisoners of war. Vladek is here when the war ends, and the prisoners are liberated in the Swiss woods. For the following days, Vladek and his companion, Shivek, go from house to house – from barns to pits – to wait and hide until the war is truly over. They finally stop at an abandoned farmhouse and help themselves to the milk and chickens before Americans arrive and liberate them.

Character summaries

Artie Spiegelman

Artie is the son of Vladek and Anja, and the character representation of Art Spiegelman, the author of *Maus*. He interviews Vladek over several years to procure his father's experiences of World War II. Artie does not get along well with Vladek, and struggles to connect with him. Artie is about thirty when he commits seriously to the project that becomes *Maus: A Survivor's Tale*.

Vladek Spiegelman

The father of Artie, Vladek is a Holocaust survivor whose story we follow throughout the novel. He is first married to Anja, then, after her death, to Mala. In his later years he is a difficult man who is incredibly stingy and racist. Vladek is thirty-three when the war begins, and sixty-eight when most of the interviewing takes place with Artie.

Anja Spiegelman

Anja is married to Vladek and is the mother of Richieu and Artie. She survives the Holocaust with Vladek. Anja is from a wealthy family and very intelligent, speaking several languages. She is fairly silent in the novel due to the fact that Artie does not know much about her wartime experiences, and he is unable to learn more because Vladek burnt her diaries some time ago. Anja is twenty-seven when the war begins. We learn that she killed herself in 1968, when she was fifty-six and Artie was twenty.

Richieu Spiegelman

The first son of Vladek and Anja, Richieu is born soon after the couple marry. At the age of five or six, he is sent away to live with Tosha, Anja's sister, for his safety. However, Tosha poisons him to prevent him from being killed by the Germans.

Mala Spiegelman

Mala is married to Vladek. She is also a survivor of the Holocaust. Mala knew Vladek and Anja before the war, and in the course of the novel we learn about Mala's family dying in the war. Through her we understand that every survivor has their own story about the trauma they and their families experienced.

Françoise Mouly

The wife of author/cartoonist Art Spiegelman, Françoise acts as a sounding board for Artie as he creates *Maus*. She shares a connection with Vladek that seems to be based on quiet mutual respect; we find out that she converted to Judaism prior to marrying Artie in order to please Vladek.

Tosha Zylberberg

Anja's sister flees Sosnowiec with the children of the family, including Richieu, in order to save them from being sent to Auschwitz. She does not survive, as she poisons herself and the children when the Germans arrive.

Mr and Mrs Zylberberg

Before the war, Anja's parents are the millionaire owners of a hosiery factory in Poland. They assist Vladek in purchasing his own factory, and they take care of Richieu while Vladek accompanies Anja to the sanatorium. Yet, as Vladek reflects, even their wealth does not save their lives, as they too are sent to Auschwitz.

Lucia Greenberg

Lucia is one of Vladek's early girlfriends. Vladek reflects, 'Her family was nice, but had no money' (p.17, frame 3). When he ends his relationship with Lucia and begins dating Anja, Lucia is distraught, and writes to Anja in an attempt to break the couple up.

Mrs Kawka

Friends of Vladek's connect him with Mrs Kawka, who hides Vladek and Anja in her barn. A stern woman, she makes it clear that should Vladek and Anja be found, they must pretend they do not know her. She provides shelter until they are taken in by Mrs Motonowa.

Mrs Motonowa

A Polish woman who works on the black market in Sosnowiec, Mrs Motonowa offers Vladek and Anja refuge in her cellar, and Anja tutors her son while staying with her. Mrs Motonowa gets spooked after the Germans take her goods, so she sends Vladek and Anja away. After a time on the streets, Vladek runs into Mrs Motonowa, who feels guilty for casting them out and offers temporary refuge again.

Haskel Spiegelman

Haskel is a chief of the Jewish police who takes bribes from Jews to smuggle them away from danger. Vladek refers to him as a 'kombinator', a 'schemer … a crook' (p.118, frame 3). The jewellery that is given to Haskel to smuggle Anja's parents out of Sosnowiec does not save them from capture.

Shivek

Shivek is a friend of Vladek's from before the war. They find one another in Auschwitz and become companions once the war is over and they are freed by the Americans.

Pavel

Artie's psychiatrist, Pavel, is a Czech Jew who also survived the Holocaust – he was in the concentration camps Terezin and Auschwitz. Pavel assists Artie in making sense of how he feels about his father's experiences.

Yidl

Yidl is a Russian Jew who is chief of the tinsmiths in Auschwitz. Vladek is initially afraid of him, but gives him food rations to keep him on side.

BACKGROUND & CONTEXT

Art Spiegelman's conceptualisation of *Maus* began in 1972, when he decided to do a comic strip about racism based on stories his father, Vladek, had told him during childhood. In this comic strip, Spiegelman depicted Jews as mice and Nazi Germans as cats. When Spiegelman took the strip to show his father, Vladek divulged more of his story about the Holocaust, and Spiegelman decided to interview him further to glean more of his story. By the time Spiegelman moved to New York in 1975, he had decided to do 'a very long comic book' based on the interviews he had conducted with his father, along with additional research. In 1978 he carried out further interviews and collected enough material to complete the project. From December 1980, the comic strips were serialised in *RAW*; the magazine featured a chapter of the story in every issue until 1991. In 1986, the publisher Pantheon published the first six chapters as *Maus: A Survivor's Tale* (subtitled *My Father Bleeds History*). In 1991, Pantheon published the last five chapters of Part Two as *And Here My Troubles Began*. Both volumes were brought together in 1994, when the Voyager Company released *The Complete Maus* on CD-ROM.

Comic books as literature

When we think of comic books, we could be forgiven for thinking in the first instance of superhero and fantasy comics, made famous by the likes of comic-book giants DC Comics and Marvel. We know that a comic book is a story (usually fictional) told through a sequence of frames or pictures, within which characters engage in dialogue. The comic book traditionally has little prose, and the reader derives most of the story from the visual frames and the dialogue. It is this dialogue, along with brief captions in the frames that provide some narration, that delivers the plot.

The most notable comic-book publishers, DC Comics and Marvel, are no doubt part of the reason why comics are often regarded as juvenile or non-literary. Rising to great popularity in the 1950s and 1960s, superhero comic books aimed primarily at younger readers dominated the shelves. As a result of this popularity, most considered the comic book as a genre rather than a medium for literary regard. It is only in recent years that comic books have been categorised as 'graphic novels' when they present serious or real stories beyond the adolescent fantasies often associated with comic books.

Underground comix

In his retrospective of comics, *Co-Mix*, Spiegelman provides a definition of comix as a verb: 'To mix together. As in words and pictures' (Spiegelman 2013, p.7). What sets comix apart from comic books is that the content or nature of comix is usually socially relevant or satirical.

When we refer to something as 'underground', it suggests a movement away from the mainstream or popular. Underground media in any form is typically published or exhibited on a small scale, outside of large corporate publishers or distributors. It often pushes boundaries, incorporating content that would not be permitted in mainstream publications or exhibits, including coarse language and gritty depictions of drug use, sexuality and violence.

The underground comix movement was most popular in the late 1960s to early 1970s in the United States, and Art Spiegelman was a prominent player in it. His autobiographical comix, 'Prisoner on the Hell Planet: A Case History', which was published 'in an obscure underground comic book' (p.101, frame 8), is referred to in *Maus*: Vladek reads it and is affected by the grim yet honest account of his son's response to Anja's suicide.

Communism in Poland

In *Maus*, communists are portrayed negatively. We see this in Chapter Two of Part One, when Anja is suspected of being a communist and the Spiegelman house is searched by police. Anja has a neighbouring seamstress hide a package containing documents that implicate her as a communist sympathiser, and the seamstress is jailed for possession of the documents.

Communism was outlawed in Poland after World War I. The reasons for the outlawing of and subsequent negativity towards communism are complicated, owing to a long history of political turmoil in Poland, and in Europe in general. More specifically, they are a result of hundreds of years of struggle between Poland and what is now known as Russia (formerly the Union of Soviet Socialist Republics, or the Soviet Union). Power struggles between these two countries pepper their histories, with Poland once occupying Moscow (in 1610), and, more significantly, the communist Soviet Union occupying a large proportion of Poland in the nineteenth and early twentieth centuries.

Prior to World War II, when the German threat was building in Poland, Soviet Union leader Joseph Stalin made many offers to Poland to form an anti-German alliance. Poland feared Stalin's communism as much as they feared Hitler's Nazism, and they refused. Many people have argued that World War II would not have been so devastating for Poland had they allied with the Soviet Union. The truth of this will never be known. Yet in 1939 a non-aggression pact (the Molotov–Ribbentrop Pact) was signed between the Soviet Union and Germany, after the Soviet Union's alliance offers to Poland were refused. This pact contained an agreement to segment Europe, including Poland, between the two powers and was the basis of the invasion of many countries in Europe.

The Jewish people in Poland

Maus is a story about Polish Jews, and it is important to understand the distinction between Jewish people of different nations in Europe. Jews have been in Poland for centuries; for much of this time, dating back to before the year 1000, Poland was home to the largest Jewish community in Europe. Poland was known as the most tolerant country in the continent, with a long period of statutory religious tolerance and social autonomy. These laws were in place until 1772, when the partitioning of Poland began. Yet this culture of tolerance prevailed; when Poland gained political autonomy in 1918, after World War I, over 3 million Jews were residing in the country.

Before World War II, approximately 9.5 million Jews – more than sixty per cent of the world's Jewish population – lived in Europe. This equated to about two per cent of the total European population at that time. Most Jews lived in Eastern Europe (in countries including Poland, the Soviet Union, Romania, Latvia, Lithuania and Estonia), followed by central Europe (Germany, Hungary, Czechoslovakia and Austria).

The Jewish population of Poland was devastated by World War II. Historians have estimated that the number of surviving Jews in Poland was a meagre 350,000. This devastation and loss is made very real at the conclusion of Vladek's story when, in his words, 'All what is left, it's the photos' (p.275, frame 7) of Anja's family, and 'Nothing [is] left, not even a snapshot' (p.276, frame 7) of his own family.

GENRE, STRUCTURE & LANGUAGE

Genre

Maus does not fit neatly into a particular genre. The novel is constructed using three narrative levels, and with this in mind we can attempt to categorise the various genres on which the novel draws: graphic novel, biography and autobiography.

Graphic novel

Maus is often described as a graphic novel. This term first arose in the 1970s to describe socially relevant and realistic stories presented in comic-book form (as was the trend of the comix movement at this time). A graphic novel will typically have more narrative breadth than a traditional comic, in which episodes are usually centred on a protagonist and their dealings with an antagonist. A graphic novel will likely provide the reader with a narrative that has the scope and scale of a traditional prose novel.

Graphic novels use 'frame storytelling', conveying aspects of movement and fluidity visually, frame by frame, much like a film storyboard translates the movement of characters in a film script. Indeed, some graphic novels, such as Frank Miller's *Sin City*, have been used in place of film storyboards, as their detail and sophistication can surpass that of the film storyboard. Through this frame storytelling, the reader is able to visualise the characters' movement, as well as the progress of characters as they interact with one another. Spiegelman also uses this frame storytelling to emphasise emotion and significant plot points. For example, the drama and gravity of Tosha's decision to poison herself and the children are emphasised with three successive frames that keep a close focus on her face, detailing the determined lines in her face and the beads of sweat on her brow, and signifying her anger and resolve (p.111, frames 5, 6 and 7).

Due to their visual component, graphic novels can present nuance that would not otherwise be apparent in a novel. In *Maus*, Spiegelman utilises visual techniques to allow his reader to see the blurring between two narrative levels or chronologies: Artie's witnessing his father's storytelling many years after the war, and Vladek's Holocaust story itself. Visual palimpsests (the layering of one image over another) are used when Vladek is telling Artie a detail from his story: a visual representation of the past that he is describing bleeds into, or overlaps with, the visual representation of the present. This is seen in Chapter Three of Part Two, where Vladek, Artie and Françoise are driving, and the bodies of prisoners can be seen hanging from the trees outside their car. Vladek tells us, 'They hanged a long, long time' (p.239, frame 7), and this, coupled with the image of the past overlayed in the present, shows us that in Vladek's mind, they are still hanging – still haunting him. Such visual palimpsests are only made possible by the novel's graphic form, and they provide us with seamless transitions between past and present.

Biography

Maus is also a complex biographical 'survivor's tale', a historical account of the Jewish Holocaust. On one level, it is a story about a man's plight during World War II, including his incarceration in Auschwitz and his ultimate survival of the Jewish genocide. Yet because a trusted familial scribe (Art Spiegelman) has procured the account from the source (Vladek) and then reproduced it, we are provided with something other than a straight biography or an autobiography.

Spiegelman thus gives us another kind of palimpsest, in that the Holocaust story is superimposed over the narrative of himself extracting his father's story. One cannot exist without the other: Artie would not have a story to tell without his father, and Vladek would not be telling his story without his son. In essence, what occurs is a mediation, in that Artie is a presence in his father's biography, prompting and assisting him in his relaying of information. A result of this mediation is that

Spiegelman does what he can to counter the unreliable nature of Vladek's memory and the problems associated with recounting history: rendered notices, maps and diagrams are included as a means to provide some objective material for the reader to appreciate that the novel is, on one level, a non-fictional biography.

Autobiography

In another sense, *Maus* is quite obviously an autobiography, because it is an account of a portion of the author's life: in particular, of the many interviews that the author conducts with his father. *Maus* thus tells the story of the complex connection between father and son. Through Artie's difficulties in interviewing his father and creating *Maus*, the reader comes to understand the long-lasting effects that World War II had not only on Artie's father, but also on Artie himself. The result is an intensely self-conscious narrative that reconstructs history as much as it retells it.

Structure

Maus is a non-fictional story that begins in Poland in 1935 and ends in New York in 1991. The reader is presented with three levels of narrative:

- a wartime account, told by the elderly Vladek
- a reconstruction narrative, where we learn of the process that Spiegelman undertook to understand (and draw) Vladek's life before and during the war
- Spiegelman's story of connecting with his father and reflecting on the experience of writing and drawing the novel. We dive in and out of the past as we learn – with Spiegelman – of his father's past.

It is worth noting that these three levels of narrative correspond with the three genres into which *Maus* can be placed.

In order to best understand how these levels contribute to the novel's structure, we should assess their relationship with each other in the narrative continuum. The first (or inner) narrative, and perhaps the main story, is that of Vladek's wartime experiences. This narrative is the root of the entire project: it is because of this story that the others are in existence. The second (middle) narrative is the discourse that takes place between Artie and his father. The reader witnesses this through Artie's interviews with his father, which he is conducting in order to create his project, *Maus*. Aligning, at times, with this middle narrative is the third (outer) narrative, in which we see the author/cartoonist Art Spiegelman reporting and reflecting on the process of creating this project. We are privy to Spiegelman's thoughts on the process, and we are made aware of his concerns about being faithful to the trauma of an event that he never experienced directly.

We should note that the second and third narrative levels overlay the first, the wartime story of *Maus*. Here there is a blurring of literary boundaries – the reader follows a compelling and devastating story of survival in perhaps the most horrific and shocking event in modern history, but they are also given a story about the process of obtaining this account, and then a reflection on this process. Spiegelman is candid in presenting Artie's experiences in interviewing Vladek: the reader witnesses all the anguish and stress Artie felt throughout the meetings. Artie struggles with a man who at times appears to be an attention-seeker, and Spiegelman goes to great lengths to share with the reader all of Vladek's digressive lamentations and paranoid ramblings. In showing this fraught relationship, Spiegelman allows his reader to experience – as he does – the phenomenon of survivor guilt that is no doubt felt by all survivors of the Holocaust, and which extends even to the children of those who survived.

Language

The language of *Maus* is thoughtful and reflective. At times it is extremely sincere, to the point where the reader may question the genuineness of the voice; at other times it is dramatic to the point of annoyance.

Through the language, Spiegelman gives his reader a number of cues that can assist in understanding the plot, voice and levels of narrative. It is through the language that we are able to comprehend aspects of the characters' motivations, their relationships with one another and, most importantly, their place in each narrative level.

Visually, the text changes depending on which level of the narrative we are following. In the third narrative level – Art Spiegelman's reflections on Vladek's account and on Artie's relationship with his father – the text is presented in sentence case: both upper- and lower-case letters. This is different from the rest of the novel, where both dialogue and Vladek's narration are in upper case. The purpose of this is to flag for the reader that we are witnessing a reflective process: Spiegelman is reflecting on the process of constructing his novel, and making the reader aware of some of his authorial choices as well as the physical and emotional processes this involved.

Another language feature is the employment of Vladek's broken English. When Vladek engages in dialogue in the wartime narrative, the language is written using correct syntax, grammar and vocabulary. This is particularly noticeable alongside the broken English in the second narrative level – both in his dialogue with Artie and in the narration he provides for his wartime story. This is a sophisticated way to alert the reader to the fact that we are dealing with translations and stories spanning not only time but also place. The use of language is perhaps showing us something about the geography: when Vladek is in Poland, he would be using Polish – a language in which he is fluent – to speak with those around him. This is evident both before and during the war – whomever Vladek comes across speaks to him in Polish, unless it is otherwise stated. When Vladek is in the United States, he uses his fractured English, as seen in his dialogue with Artie, Françoise and Mala.

CHAPTER-BY-CHAPTER ANALYSIS

Prologue (Rego Park, New York City, 1958) (pp.5–6)

Summary: *Ten- or eleven-year old Artie is playing with friends; he falls and gets left behind. When he goes to his father, Vladek, for consolation, he does not receive it.*

When Artie approaches Vladek, the father doesn't appear to notice his son's distress. Instead, he asks Artie to assist him with sawing, only then asking why he is crying, following it up straight away with, 'Hold better on the wood' (p.6, frame 2). Note that no physical comfort is given to Artie.

While it is unclear whether Vladek's indifference is due to his disinterest in his son or an inability to comfort him, this section certainly marks the tenor of the relationship between Artie and Vladek. It also suggests that from a young age Artie is aware of something of the darkness of his father's past. Artie did not experience the Holocaust, but he certainly experiences its emotional aftermath. Art Spiegelman has said that living with parents who endured the war was his own Holocaust.

Key point

The prologue is an important section of the novel because it sets up the relationship between father and son. Both Artie and Vladek are shown here to be vulnerable, and their individual struggles are alluded to: while Vladek seems jaded by his past, Artie is affected by his present, seemingly unsure of how to fit in to or make sense of a world with cruelty.

Part One: My Father Bleeds History

Chapter One: The Sheik (pp.11–25)

Summary: *Artie visits Vladek and discusses the book about Vladek's life that he wishes to draw. Vladek describes his early adult life and how he became engaged to Anja.*

Vladek begins to tell the story of his life, reflecting on being young, attractive and successful – 'a nice, handsome boy' (p.15, frame 1). These are attributes that, tragically, are later ended by Vladek's 'troubles' throughout the war. Artie tells us that he and his father are not 'close' (p.13, frame 1), and we certainly feel the tension between the pair as the sequence of interviews begins.

Key point

Vladek rides his exercise bike while telling his life story. This bike recurs throughout the novel, and it provides the reader with a symbolic representation of the events he describes. Vladek is physically working hard towards no known destination – a visual metaphor for his horrible experiences in Nazi concentration camps.

Note the use of pictures and framing in this chapter. Artie picks up a framed photograph, but we do not know who is in the picture. In the next panel, Vladek's arms frame Artie, with the photograph on the right. Finally, Artie tells his father to 'Start with Mom ... Tell me how you met' (p.14, frame 6), pointing at the photograph. Not only does this focus on the mystery that is Anja's story, but it also shows us early on that Spiegelman will use visual cues and framing as part of his storytelling. In depicting Artie within the frame of Vladek's arms, Spiegelman is reflecting on the fact that Artie is framed by his father's story; a part of who Artie is can be defined by who his father is, and what he has experienced.

Vladek's relationship with his second wife, Mala, is particularly telling of his impatience with others. Artie tells us that Vladek and Mala 'didn't get along' (p.13, frame 6), and this is evident in Vladek's consistent nagging at and complaints about her.

This chapter establishes Artie as the faithful scribe of his family's history, while representing Vladek as a neurotic character who is frustratingly self-centred. Vladek proudly tells Artie, 'People always told me I looked just like Rudolph Valentino' (p.15, frame 5). Valentino was a famous actor from the silent-movie period. *The Sheik* is a 1921 silent film starring Rudolph Valentino, in which the protagonist, a determined and cunning sheik, is hired to escort a headstrong woman in the Middle East. This is an interesting comparison for Vladek to bring up, because an Arabic sheikh is an honourable leader of his people. Presumably, Vladek enjoys this likeness to a notable and honourable member of society.

The chapter ends with Vladek telling Artie that he doesn't want him to write about Lucia, Vladek's former girlfriend, because it 'isn't so proper, so respectful' (p.25, frame 5). It appears that Vladek wants only admirable qualities to be depicted in the book – Vladek has experienced much disrespect and dishonour in his life, and so perhaps does not want to be the cause of this himself or have it reflected to him.

Q Why do you think Spiegelman chooses to begin the story of Vladek's life with the period when he was 'young, and really a nice, handsome boy'?

Q How does Spiegelman show early in the narrative that Artie's relationship with Vladek is a difficult one?

Chapter Two: The Honeymoon (pp.27–42)

Summary: *When Artie visits his father to obtain more of his story, Vladek is agitated and anxious. He tells of the early stages of his marriage to Anja and the rise of Nazism in Europe in the 1930s.*

Artie's visit begins with Vladek counting his pills, speaking of how terrible his condition is. Vladek tells Artie, 'For my condition I must fight to *save* myself' (p.28, frame 5), which calls into question the mental awareness of a man who actually did, once, have to fight to save his life. This comment is bookended at the conclusion of the chapter, when Vladek drops his pills and complains about his poor eyesight, telling Artie, 'You see how I have to suffer?' (p.41, frame 5). Honour and dignity are very important to Vladek, as seen when he tells of not wanting to embarrass his doctor for not recognising that he has one glass eye.

In his retelling, Vladek reveals that he and Anja have a son, Richieu. We see that Anja is susceptible to mental illness: the birth sends her into a severe bout of depression, and she is treated at a sanatorium for three months. After their return, Vladek finds out that he must go to war and serve Poland on the front. All these events are indeed far from the 'honeymoon' claimed in this chapter's title. Here, Spiegelman uses irony, depicting the opposite of what one would expect or hope – an experience that Vladek would have had time and time again in his life.

Key point

Note how Spiegelman depicts the rise of Nazism. On page 35 in frame 5, the Swastika rises like a sun over the town in Germany, with the banner announcing, 'This town is Jew free.' Spiegelman depicts the gradual rise of Nazism subtly – icons and images are inserted here and there, but not particularly explicitly. It is on this same page where we first see Nazi Germans, depicted as cats. Note the particularly menacing and skeletal, scary faces of the Germans in frames 3 and 4.

Q What do we learn about Vladek from his insistence on counting and apportioning his pills?

Chapter Three: Prisoner of War (pp.43–71)

Summary: *Artie visits his father frequently to get more information about his past. Vladek tells Artie of his short time on the war front, fighting against Germany, and then of his time in prisoner-of-war camps, and his eventual release.*

Vladek tells of how, during his time as a soldier fighting for Poland, he questioned, 'Why should I kill anyone?' (p.50, frame 2). This shows us Vladek's moral compass: even though he is in a war, serving his country, he does not see the point in killing people. He does eventually kill a soldier. Yet it is interesting to note that, despite all his ill treatment and the terrible things that prisoners throughout the war had to do to survive, after this shooting, Vladek does not harm anybody else during the war.

We see the obvious segregation and persecution of the Jews once Vladek is taken prisoner, as the non-Jewish prisoners are given better conditions in the camp. While in 1939 Adolf Hitler's Final Solution had not yet begun (the killing of European Jews was yet to start on the massive scale seen in the concentration camps), the poorer conditions in which the Jewish prisoners were kept signals the beginning of their persecution in Vladek's story. Vladek tells of how prisoners were made to 'move mountains' (p.58, frame 1), indicating the impossible scale of the labour that prisoners had to carry out in these camps.

Note the fine detail with which Spiegelman draws Vladek's grandfather's hand on page 59 (frame 3). This shows us that, even though Spiegelman uses the metaphor of cats and mice for Nazis and Jews respectively, there is humanity clearly depicted. The details of lines and wrinkles in the grandfather's hand signify the wisdom and guidance of the great-grandfather Artie never knew.

Artie plays an important role in the construction of Vladek's story, prompting his father for facts and details as his story progresses. This is significant, not only as it demonstrates the frailty of human memory, but also as it shows that Artie and Vladek are both essential to this process; without either one, we would not have a story. We are also given a map of Poland. Such information is a reminder to the reader that while we are reading a comic, the story is essentially factual.

Key point

Faith is important in this chapter. Faith is no doubt something that affords Vladek much of the strength he has in order to continue during the war. Vladek's dream of his grandfather marks a significant moment for him, as it is from here that Parshas Truma becomes a significant day for him and his family: his wedding to Anja falls during this week, as does Artie's birth. Indeed, soldiers do arrive on the day of Parshas Truma, assuring the prisoners that they will be released and taken back to Sosnowiec.

Q Vladek often seems as outraged by relatively trivial things in the present (cigarette ash on the carpet, Mala's preoccupation with money) as he is by the horrors of war. How does this shape the reader's view of Vladek?

Chapter Four: The Noose Tightens (pp.73–95)

Summary: *After Vladek's return from the war, conditions in Poland grow worse. Jewish Poles are made to move from ghetto to ghetto, and some are sent to Auschwitz. Mala tells Artie of her family's survival of Auschwitz.*

Vladek tells of the living conditions in Sosnowiec dramatically worsening; as the chapter's title suggests, the metaphorical noose tightens on Vladek and the Zylberbergs. Despite this, Vladek shows that he is a clever operator. He thinks quickly and strategically, but he is also clearly a very lucky man. On page 79 he manages to make money by acquiring cloth and selling it to a friend, and he says that he learnt during this time how to do things that proved 'useful' (p.80, frame 8) to him in Auschwitz. He manages to escape capture a couple of times, partly due to luck and partly due to skill. It is because Vladek works as a carpenter that he is spared being taken to Auschwitz in the gruelling Dienst Stadium selection.

We see in this chapter, again, that Artie acts as mediator in the novel: he prompts his father and urges him to keep on track. This is an important narrative function, as it shows us Vladek's dependency on Artie, and through this we can understand that Vladek may not be an entirely faithful or reliable narrator of the story. When Vladek is about to tell how Tosha Zylberberg takes Richieu and the other children with her to the Zawiercie ghetto, Artie interjects, saying, '*Please*, Dad, if you don't keep your story chronological, I'll never get it straight ...' (p.84, frame 1). On the same page, we see a drawing of the order mandating all Jews in Sosnowiec relocate to Stara Sosnowiec. This shows us that Spiegelman is indeed an active participant in reconstructing his father's story. Through his involvement, we are able to make sense of Vladek's story.

Darkness is used as a visual cue in this chapter, as are storyboard conventions of movement and flow. We see the first signs of real brutality towards the Jews, and Vladek says that they finally 'believed' (p.90, frame 3) the stories that were surfacing about the horrors of Auschwitz. In order to convey this important change in tone, Spiegelman uses shading to depict the evils that are being committed and the subsequent darkness felt by its victims. When Vladek and the Zylberbergs move to Stara Sosnowiec, they are represented as dark silhouettes, with the white snowfall dotting their bodies (p.84, frame 3). In addition, Vladek is shown in darkness when he is haunted by the bodies of the Jews that were hanged; the faces of the corpses hovering above his head reflect the anguish haunting him (p.86, frame 1). Note the position of the legs of the hanged Jews in frames 3, 4 and 5 on page 85; we can visualise the movement of the bodies through the changes in position, providing a haunting, affecting image. Further, when Vladek tells Artie how his family had to deliver Anja's grandparents to the Germans, Vladek and Artie are depicted in silhouette, demonstrating the significantly bleak turn of the story (p.89).

Also note Spiegelman's framing of the family in this chapter. On page 76 we look into the family's meal together, with the panes of the window providing their own smaller frames of the different members of Vladek and Anja's family. In the following frames on the same page, snapshots are provided of each grouping on this table as Vladek describes these people in more detail. This whole page is bookended at the top left and bottom right corners by Vladek, on his bike, telling his story.

The chapter concludes with Mala's conversation with Artie. Through Mala, we learn of Vladek's father's potential fate, as she tells how her own mother was 'taken' (p.94, frame 3) and made to live in suffocatingly cramped conditions before ending up in Auschwitz. Mala's involvement in the story is important, as through her we obtain some detail as to what happened after the Dienst Stadium selection (detail of the fate of loved ones was a luxury very few people had), and through her presence in the narrative we understand that everyone has a story to tell about the war – Vladek's is only one of many.

Q What is the significance of Artie complaining, '*Please*, Dad, if you don't keep your story chronological, I'll never get it straight ...'? How important is Artie's role in his father's story?

Chapter Five: Mouse Holes (pp.97–129)

Summary: *When Artie next visits his father, he learns that Vladek has read an old comic that Artie wrote about his mother's suicide. Vladek describes the worsening conditions in Poland and how he and Anja avoided deportation to Auschwitz.*

We learn more of Vladek's neuroticism in this chapter: he is depicted as a difficult man whom Artie struggles to deal with and tolerate – shown in Artie's refusal to help him fix a drainpipe.

In this chapter, Vladek tells of the lengths that people went to in order to attempt to save their own lives and the lives of those they loved. The 'tragedy among tragedies' (p.111, frame 9) of Richieu's death is that there was simply no escape for some people, and, despite Vladek and Anja sending their son away in the hope that he would be spared, Richieu becomes the youngest victim of war in Vladek's family.

Vladek's smarts and cunning are also notable in this chapter, as it is through his ability to build bunkers in the houses in which they stayed that he and the Zylberbergs are able to avoid deportation to Auschwitz for a little while. This chapter also shows the value of knowing the right people: through Haskel and Miloch, Vladek gets jobs within the ghetto, and he avoids being killed because he is a relative of the popular Haskel.

In this chapter we can appreciate the unique aspect that the comic form gives this story. Through the frames, Spiegelman is able to offer more than just a visual representation of his characters and their story. For example, while telling Artie about the bunker that he built to hide in, Vladek grabs Artie's notebook, saying, 'It's good to know exactly how was it – just in case' (p.112, frame 6), and we then have a representation of the sketch drawn in the notebook. This is followed on the next page with a visual reconstruction of this bunker – Spiegelman gives this sketch life as the bunker's layout is replicated in the layout of the frames, reinforcing the cramped living conditions. On pages 116 and 117, as Vladek's family comes under increasing strain and Anja's parents are captured, window frames are used to depict the confinement of the characters. On page 127, the path that Anja and Vladek walk forms a swastika. This imagery represents Vladek and Anja's predicament of having nowhere to go, as in Poland at this time (around 1944), all paths led to the Nazis (and to Auschwitz).

Similarly, note the framing in this chapter. When Tosha decides to poison herself and the children, we understand that this awful decision is made with determination and anguish: Spiegelman depicts Tosha's decision over three consecutive frames (p.111, frames 5, 6 and 7), the final frame focusing on her face, with her stern eyes and sweat on her forehead. This illustrates that Tosha is a strong woman who will not die on anybody else's terms. Similarly, when Vladek is consoling the grieving Anja (p.124, frames 7, 8 and 9), the frames focus on the couple's faces as Vladek delivers his poignant message: that 'To die, it's *easy*' (frame 7). Here, Spiegelman uses a visual palimpsest again, but in this case he layers the present over the past, with frame 10 depicting Vladek in a similar pose, though years later, telling the story to his son.

Key point

Spiegelman's inclusion of his comic 'Prisoner on the Hell Planet' is an example of his telling his own history in the novel. This is the only account that we have of Anja from Spiegelman himself. The style of the drawings shows the anguish that Spiegelman was clearly experiencing at the time: characters (including him) are dark and overbearing, with exhausted, lined faces. In addition, the Artie in this comic is wearing a striped prison outfit, no doubt similar to that worn by his parents in Auschwitz.

We are encouraged to consider whether this outfit is a conscious likeness, or a representation of his feeling like a prisoner to the emotional turmoil of his depression and his mother's suicide. Note that this comic within a comic has a black border that runs to the edge of the page (into what is known as the bleed) and is visible even when the novel is closed. This bleeding of darkness perhaps indicates how his mother's suicide has bled into other aspects of his life and affected him profoundly. A link can be drawn to the title of the part, with its reference to 'bleeding' history.

Q How do you see the suicidal actions of Anja and Tosha as they are depicted in this chapter? Do you see one more favourably than the other? Or are they each, in their own way, an innocent victim of the holocaust?

Chapter Six: Mouse Trap (pp.131–61)

Summary: *Vladek tells Artie how he and Anja go from property to property, hiding from the Germans. Eventually they are betrayed by smugglers, captured and sent to Auschwitz. Artie learns that his father burned his mother's diaries.*

This is the last chapter of Part I of *Maus*, and it marks the end of Vladek's time leading up to Auschwitz.

At the beginning of this chapter, Mala expresses her frustrations with Vladek. It is clear that he is a very difficult man, but we know that his present-day frugality and pragmatism are products of having survived the war. We see more of his wartime difficulties in this chapter.

While many people are able to help Vladek and Anja, such as Mrs Kawka and Mrs Motonowa, they do so at great risk to themselves and their families. This shows the profound difficulty felt by all during the war. Even though Polish non-Jews were not being killed systematically, as the Jews were, Poland as a whole was still struggling under Hitler's rule. As such, it was incredibly dangerous for Poles to go against Hitler and his Nazi regime. As readers of *Maus* we are not necessarily supposed to be scathing of those who are reluctant to help Jewish Poles, or even of those who betray them, such as the smugglers. The war was difficult and potentially deadly for everyone, and as Vladek notes, 'It was everybody to take care for *himself!*' (p.116, frame 5).

Note that when the characters are attempting to hide the fact that they are Jewish, Spiegelman draws them wearing pig masks to fit in with Polish non-Jews. Vladek tells us that this concealment of identity was not easy for Anja, as she clearly looked Jewish; Spiegelman shows us this with her inability to conceal her tail (p.138). Later, when the couple are found by the Germans, their masks are removed, with their true identities revealed.

When Vladek and Anja arrive at Auschwitz, we feel the darkness and horror of this scene. Although they reach the camp in a white landscape in the middle of winter (we can see ice on the 'Arbeit macht frei' sign), there is much darkness, and the foreboding chimneys billow smoke over the camp. This reflects the general atmosphere and mood. Vladek's comment, 'And we knew that from here we will not come out anymore' (p.159, frame 4), is significant, as it foreshadows that they will never truly 'come out' from the horror of Auschwitz emotionally.

Key point

When Vladek tells Artie that he no longer has Anja's diaries, Artie calls him a 'murderer' (p.161, frames 4 and 9). This is because, in burning the only potential for connection that Artie could have to his mother's wartime story, Vladek ultimately kills her memory. The significance of Vladek's actions cannot be ignored. Anja may have survived the ovens of Auschwitz, but her only existing record has been incinerated. What we have here is a bleakly literal repetition of the Holocaust, where Vladek does to Anja's belongings what his persecutors did to the millions of victims.

Q Do you blame Vladek for destroying Anja's diaries? What is the effect of their absence on the narrative of *Maus*?

Part Two: And Here My Troubles Began

Chapter One: Mauschwitz (pp.169–97)

Summary: *Mala leaves Vladek, and Artie and Françoise stay with him for a short time. Artie reflects on growing up with parents who survived the Holocaust. Vladek tells Artie of his integration into Auschwitz and of how he befriended a Kapo.*

We see Vladek's neuroticism and demanding nature again in this chapter, as he pretends to have a heart attack in order to get Artie to phone him back. We feel Artie's frustration, and this is brought to the fore when he reflects to Françoise on the difficulty of his childhood. He divulges that if faced with the decision to send one of his parents to the ovens of Auschwitz, he would send his father, which gives us an indication of the turmoil that Vladek has inflicted on Artie's life. It also shows the longing that Artie has for his mother.

More importantly, Artie's fantasies of Zyklon B (the pesticide used to gas victims in Auschwitz) coming out of his showerhead, and his guilt in 'having had an easier life' than his parents, are indications of the second-hand trauma experienced by second-generation Holocaust survivors. Artie is conflicted about how he feels about both his parents, and he candidly admits to feeling 'inadequate' (p.176, frame 6) in the shadow of their suffering.

The fluidity with which Spiegelman visually re-creates the scene of Artie and Françoise driving, with their candid conversation about Artie's feelings, is worthy of note. He uses a series of close-ups and long shots to contrast the traffic they are moving through with the deep emotional reflection taking place within the car. Significantly, Artie tells Françoise that 'reality is too *complex* for comics' (p.176, frame 6), yet this reflection, the reality of admitting the difficulty of his project, is quite profound. This is coupled with the fact that Spiegelman represents the mundane as well as the sensational reality of the Holocaust. In frame 7 on the same page, Artie says, 'In real life you'd *never* have let me talk this long without interrupting', inviting us to consider whether Françoise did indeed – in real life – allow Spiegelman to talk this long, or if this is just a nod to the reader's witnessing of the reality.

Vladek tells Artie of his first days in Auschwitz, and we see Vladek's guile surfacing again, as he is able to speak English and give the Kapo lessons. By having the Kapo's favour, Vladek is able to obtain small comforts and no doubt gain some energy (physical and emotional) that helps to keep him alive in Auschwitz.

On page 185 Spiegelman uses layout – the arrangement of frames on the page – to depict two levels of narrative: Vladek's arrival at Auschwitz and his retelling of it. The frames are arranged vertically on this page, with the left side representing one timeframe (the second narrative level, in which Vladek is telling his story) and the right representing another (the wartime narrative). The progression of the frames goes from the top down, signifying the decline in humanity that is being presented in the wartime narrative on the right as the Jews are ordered to undress and part with their belongings upon their arrival at Auschwitz.

Q The introduction of Françoise to the narrative allows for Artie to express some of his more private feelings and experiences. How does this develop our understanding of his character?

Chapter Two: Auschwitz (Time Flies) (pp.199–234)

Summary: *Vladek has died and the first volume of Maus has been published. Artie has been depressed; he visits his psychiatrist, who discusses the concept of survivor guilt. Artie listens to recordings of his interviews with his father. Vladek tells how he made contact with Anja in Auschwitz and reveals the horror of the crematoriums.*

This chapter is important as it reveals the gruelling process that Artie is undertaking in creating the novel, and also how conflicted he feels about creating it when his father endured so much worse than what Artie is going through. Artie presents life achievements of his own alongside those of his father in Auschwitz (p.201), and we can feel the anguish and guilt that Artie is experiencing as a result of dredging up his father's past.

The depiction of Artie as a little boy in the following pages shows how he feels weighed down and belittled by the gravity of guilt pressing upon him, as well as the fact that he feels deprived of a boyhood with his father – a representation of Artie feeling arrested in development. Images of dead bodies pepper his reality; they are ghosts of his father's past cluttering the path he walks. He reveals that the sessions with his psychiatrist, Pavel, 'somehow make [him] feel better' (p.206, frame 9), and while saying this, he grows man-sized again, frame by frame.

In Artie's session with Pavel – who is also a survivor of the Holocaust – they both wear masks as they play the role of Jewish men in Artie's book; Spiegelman does not deviate from his metaphor of Jews as mice. There are some rather profound moments of truth in this exchange, and Pavel is clearly a very valuable guide for Artie as he grapples with the difficulty of writing about his father's past. Note the large speech bubble Spiegelman gives Pavel on page 204, frame 8, to convey the emotion with which Pavel says, 'No ... just sadness.' This piece of dialogue is surrounded by white space, signalling to us the emptiness Pavel feels as a Holocaust survivor. The frame following the Samuel Beckett quote, 'Every word is like an unnecessary stain on silence and nothingness' (p.205, frame 6), has no dialogue, with both characters providing the silence required to make true the Beckett quote. In this, Spiegelman tries to encourage his reader to ponder this silence for themselves.

The horrors of Auschwitz are explicit in this chapter, with death prominent in many frames. This marks the time that the devastating slaughter of millions of Hungarians was taking place. Vladek tells Artie of the 'selektions' (p.218, frame 3), and we see the very real brushes with death that Vladek has while in Auschwitz. His detailed account of the gas chambers and ovens of the crematorium buildings provide us with a gruelling history lesson on the horrific fate that met hundreds of thousands of people at Auschwitz.

In order to convey the terrible reality of the story, Spiegelman again provides us with factual detail in the form of maps and diagrams. The map of the Auschwitz complex helps us to contextualise the sheer size of the camps. Other diagrams, such as those detailing how Vladek mended shoes, or the mathematics of how to arrange contact with Anja, reiterate to us that this is a comic book in which images are powerful conveyers of meaning.

Spiegelman takes advantage of the fact that he is able to depict detail visually. He portrays the crematorium buildings as empty and lifeless. With the absence of people in these buildings, there is an absence of emotion – they appear cold and haunting, their emptiness signifying the destruction of human life that was achieved within their walls.

This is contrasted with the awful imagery and screams seen soon after, when Jews are being burned alive in the giant graves, with 'the fat from the burning bodies' being 'scooped and poured again so everyone could burn better' (p.232, frame 5). Spiegelman shows here that much of the suffering was unseen and unheard, without dignity or meaning.

On page 214, Artie prompts his father when he asks about the orchestra playing at the gates of Auschwitz. When Vladek tells Artie that he does not remember any orchestra playing, the orchestra is concealed by the marching prisoners, with the instruments and conductor's baton partially visible above the heads of the prisoners. This is a visual depiction of the haze of memory – presumably there was indeed an orchestra playing at the gates of Auschwitz, as Artie has read other accounts attesting to this fact; however, by placing the prisoners over the orchestra, we understand that this is a fact that cannot be proven.

A visual palimpsest is used in this chapter, where Vladek's account interacts with the present day. When Vladek is describing the 'selektion' process, he acts out the orders given to him: '"Face left!" ... Then again: "Face left!"' (p.218, frames 5 and 6). In the next frame, the older, plumper Vladek of the present has been replaced by the gaunt, naked prisoner Vladek, with Artie replaced by a Nazi soldier giving the orders. This layering of past and present is only possible because of the visual form, giving us a very real depiction of the sheer horror Vladek experienced and indicating how easy it is for him to relive these horrors. Through this, we see that something as simple as turning to face left and then face left again spelled doom for so many.

Key point

The chapter is bookended with Artie being hounded by bugs – flies or otherwise. It would seem that flies, which hang not only around Artie but also around the rotting corpses of the dead, are a symbol of the guilt that hovers in Artie's consciousness. The flies are a powerful visual metaphor: they are not always recognised by Artie, but we can see them; in this, Spiegelman shows that they are subconscious.

Spiegelman details the eradication of millions of Jews in the gas chambers using 'Zyklon B, a pesticide' (p.231, frame 1) and then ends the chapter with Artie spraying pesticide to get rid of the 'bugs [that are] eating him alive' (p.234, frame 7). These are the same bugs that follow Artie around at the beginning of the chapter. In Artie spraying the bugs (eradicating them), Spiegelman alerts us to the fact that Artie is slowly ridding himself of the horrors that haunt him – the process of creating this novel is a cathartic and therapeutic one. Artie is freeing himself of the oppressive burden of the bugs, a symbol of death, ironically using a pesticide akin to that which haunted his parents in Auschwitz and no doubt in their lives after the war.

Q How does the first section of this chapter add to your sense of Artie as someone who is also a 'survivor'?

Chapter Three: ...And Here My Troubles Began... (pp.235–60)

Summary: *As the Allied Front draws closer to Auschwitz, the prisoners are marched to a concentration camp at Breslau, Germany. They are held in a cattle train for weeks, and many die before being taken to a barracks, where Vladek contracts typhus.*

Even though the prisoners escape the horrors of Auschwitz, this chapter shows us that the cruelty inflicted upon them by the Germans continued for weeks thereafter, with Vladek partaking in the infamous death marches that saw hundreds of thousands of prisoners marched between camps in the middle of winter. We know that Vladek is clever, and this no doubt contributes to his ability to stay alive. He manages to conserve his energy and remain comparatively healthy (relative to his fellow prisoners) by rationing food and resting when others cannot. He makes friends who remain loyal to him by giving him food and assisting him when he is sick. When locked in the train (the cramped conditions of which are shown by the narrow, dark frames at the bottom of p.245), Vladek hangs a blanket on the cattle hooks from the roof, enabling him to rest 'and breathe a little' (p.245, frame 6). This also enables him to reach the snow on the roof of the train and hydrate himself.

Spiegelman uses the supermarket visit that Artie, Françoise and Vladek make to highlight the lasting effects that frugality and hoarding have had on Vladek. In a rather comical section of the novel, Vladek insists on taking half-eaten boxes of food back to the supermarket to get some money back. This indicates that, as Artie notes to Françoise, 'in some ways [Vladek] *didn't* survive' (p.250, frame 2), in that he still lives as though he is a prisoner, scrimping and saving to the frustration and embarrassment of those close to him.

Past and present are also melded as Vladek describes how the prisoners who staged a revolt were hanged and remained hanging 'a long, long time' (p.239). Again using palimpsest, Spiegelman includes these prisoners still hanging in the present, showing that their ghosts and the horrors of the war still hang in the consciousness of survivors.

Key point

Note the bodies that Vladek walks over on his way to the toilet (p.255, frames 3 and 4). Mice (Jews), pigs (Poles) and cats (Germans) are all seen here, indicating that people of many races and nationalities were affected by the war. Vladek's racism is particularly jarring to the reader after this, because one would think that after all his suffering he would be tolerant to other races and people who are unfairly persecuted, but this is apparently not the case. This contributes to our struggle to like Vladek, as on the one hand we are presented with his admirable story of survival, but on the other hand he appears a frustrating racist, unsympathetic to others who struggle with persecution.

Q In what ways does Spiegelman show that Vladek's past will continue to haunt Artie as much as it did Vladek throughout his life?

Chapter Four: Saved (pp.261–77)

Summary: *Vladek tells of being taken with the other prisoners to the Swiss border to be exchanged. It is here where they receive word that the war has ended, and overnight the Germans leave them. Vladek is rescued by the Americans. He goes through photographs with Artie and reflects on all the losses of his family.*

By this stage of the novel, one certainly feels the protracted nature of the prisoners' plight. Even though the war has ended, the Germans still order them around and threaten to kill them. Even after the Germans finally leave, many prisoners are still essentially captive, as they are abandoned and left unsure of whether going out into the world will result in their recapture.

When Vladek produces the box of photographs for Artie, we (and Artie) are provided with a version of the family tree that puts into context the degree of loss that has been experienced in the Spiegelman and Zylberberg families. Vladek's family has been reduced to mere snapshots of people, memories that can only be pondered. Note that rather than including the actual photographs of his family, Spiegelman draws re-creations of the photographs to show us that these people are just shadows, and '*all* what is left, it's the photos' (p.274, frame 7). In drawing the photographs, Spiegelman does not reduce detail or truth. Note that the face of Lodz's girlfriend, Sonia, is cut out of the photograph – presumably, Lodz cut her out in the actual photograph because she left him. We learn that Vladek does not have any photographs of his own family, other than of Pinek. On this same page, Spiegelman constructs Vladek by dividing his body into four frames that mimic snapshots (frames 3, 5, 6 and 7), showing us the sad reality that much of Vladek's life is composed of snapshots, or images, of his past.

Key point

The American flag forms a backdrop as the Americans arrive (p.271, frame 8). This articulates that a certain idea of ceremony arrived with the Americans, with the flag heralding the proud and patriotic victory that marked the American involvement in the war, and their role as liberators to the survivors of the Holocaust.

Q Is anything really 'saved' in this chapter?

Chapter Five: The Second Honeymoon (pp.279–96)

Summary: *Vladek travels to New York to be closer to Artie and receive medical treatment for his lungs and heart. He tells of finally getting identity papers and being reunited with Anja in Sosnowiec.*

It is interesting to see the ailments in the past and present mirroring one another in this chapter. Vladek's current health troubles seem imagined, as he is deemed 'fine' (p.287, frame 5) after travelling to New York for treatment and is soon released. He then tells of real health trouble just after the war, when in Garmisch-Partenkirchen. Here, he has a relapse of typhoid, and later finds out that he has diabetes – very significant scars of the malnourishment and brush with death that he met with in Auschwitz.

Before he reunites with Anja, Vladek sends her a photograph of himself, dressed in the camp uniform. It is a powerful image for several reasons. Firstly, it is his sign to Anja that he is healthy and alive. Secondly, there is sad irony in the fact that a photographer will make money from people wanting to take their photograph dressed in clothing that, to many, is a sign of profound persecution, suffering and death. Yet there is a wonderful irony involved, as a healthy and defiant Vladek stares at the camera with a determined expression, indicating that he did not fall victim to this uniform; and we know that he can now take it off as he pleases and step away from everything that it represents.

In the final frames, we are invited to question Vladek's authority as narrator. We know that Vladek and Anja do not live 'happy ever after' (p.296, frame 4); at this comment we feel a certain sadness, and we are reminded that Vladek is not the faithful storyteller that we (and Artie) hope he is. In the final frame, Vladek tells Artie, whom he addresses as Richieu, that he has told '*enough* stories for now' (p.296, frame 6). In this utterance, not only do we sense Vladek's disorientation in having dredged up a gruelling and horrific past, but we also see the undercurrent of loss in his inability to differentiate between his dead son and his living son. The reader wonders if the ghosts of Vladek's past disturb him more than he has led us to believe.

Q To what extent do the final pages provide a sense of resolution to the narrative?

CHARACTERS & RELATIONSHIPS

Artie Spiegelman

Key quotes

'In some ways [Vladek is] just like the racist caricature of the miserly old Jew.' (p.133, frame 8)

'... Murderer.' (p.161, frame 9)

'Maybe EVERYONE has to feel guilty. EVERYONE! FOREVER!' (p.202, frame 4)

We see Artie and the various visits he pays his father through the lens of the author, who is sharing his experiences with us. As a result, the Artie in *Maus* is a candid and thoughtful but pained man who uses the writing and drawing of *Maus* as a means to come to terms with his own relationship with his father. He also uses the process to explore the life of parents he never wholly knew.

Most of the narrative of *Maus* fluctuates between Artie's depiction of Vladek's wartime narrative and Spiegelman's depiction of Artie's relationship with his father. It is a troubled relationship, one that is clearly wrought with guilt and irritation – for both parties. Artie is often exasperated by his father's mood swings, and struggles to tolerate the emotional inconsistencies of a man who seems so haunted by his past that he is removed from his present-day reality. Artie plays a significant role in the construction of Vladek's survival story – at times he corrects his father and guides him along in his recollections, and this is important.

Key point

Artie is entrusted with the transmission of important family history. In a way it becomes his Holocaust story too, as we see the profound effect it has on him – not only in the difficulty he has in procuring the story from his neurotic father, but also from the autobiographical reflections and discussions he has with his wife, Françoise, and psychiatrist, Pavel.

While Artie can often be seen acting distant and irritated with Vladek, he is also incredibly reflective and sensitive about his father and his plight. At the beginning of Chapter Two of Part Two, the story takes a particularly autobiographical turn when Artie is seen at his desk drawing the frames that he talks about in the dialogue within the frames. Artie is drawn sitting atop a mountain of dead Jewish bodies and divulges that he has been 'feeling depressed' (p.201, frame 5) lately. This grim and confronting depiction of the author's personal frame of mind demonstrates his insecurities, as well as the cathartic process that must be felt in constructing the novel.

We also see Artie's sensitive nature in our first introduction to him, in the novel's prologue, where we see the child Artie going to his father for comfort after being left behind by his 'friends' (p.6, frame 2). Vladek's response here is one of tough realism, suggesting that he has experienced things that *really* test one's understanding of friendship. It is clear to the reader from the story's outset that Artie lives in the shadow of the Holocaust – while he did not experience it for himself, he does experience it second-hand, via his parents. Artie obviously feels guilt about this, as we see in his confession to Françoise, when he says '… I somehow wish I had been in Auschwitz *with* my parents so I could really know what they lived through!… I guess it's *some* kind of guilt about having had an easier life than they did' (p.176, frame 3).

Vladek Spiegelman

Key quotes

'To die, it's *easy* … But you have to *struggle* for life! Until the last moment we must struggle together!' (p.124, frames 7, 8 and 9)

'And we came here to the concentration camp Auschwitz. And we knew that from here we will not come out anymore …' (p.159, frame 4)

'It's not even to *compare*. The Shvartsers and the Jews!' (p.259, frame 6)

'I'm *tired* from talking, Richieu, and it's *enough* stories for now …' (p.296, frame 6)

Vladek is Artie's father, a survivor of the Jewish Holocaust of World War II. We see Vladek through the storytelling of Artie, who visits Vladek and undertakes a series of taped interviews with him in order to learn more about his time during the war. We receive two contrasting depictions of Vladek through the multi-layered chronology of the narrative: in one, Vladek is represented via the narration of wartime events provided by Vladek himself; the second is represented via the interviews and conversations with Artie. The Vladek in the wartime narrative is a fighter: his 'survivor's tale' is a remarkable story of courage, wit and endurance. The Vladek we see during Artie's interviews is cantankerous and difficult, and complains constantly about many aspects of his life – particularly his wife, Mala.

Key point

The two depictions of Vladek serve as an illustration of how the horrors and tribulations of war change an individual, but they are also a function of storytelling: the Vladek that he describes is brave, admirable and clever; the Vladek that is drawn (literally) by Spiegelman is shaped by the author's frustrations and dealings with a difficult father.

Yet the events that occur in the wartime chronology provide a clear justification for aspects of Vladek's personality in the later chronology. We see traits in his later life that have developed as a result of the trials and suffering he has experienced. Frugality and saving things enabled Vladek to survive during the war – most notably, during his time in Auschwitz. Sacrificing food and setting aside rations in order to make bribes and deals on the black market in Auschwitz gets Vladek ahead of many and, arguably, saves his life on various occasions. It appears that this frugality remains forever in Vladek's psyche, as he seems stingy beyond reason in his life after the war. Vladek wastes nothing. This is shown, comically, when he manages to convince the manager at the Shop-Rite to take back his opened boxes of cereal in exchange for more groceries. It seems that Vladek struggles to connect with people; as Mala puts it, 'He's more attached to things than to people' (p.95, frame 6). It is made clear that to Vladek, people come and go, whereas possessions can be meaningful and sentimental, especially to a person who has had everything taken from him.

Vladek's relationship with his second wife, Mala, is intriguing. One of the first introductions we have to Vladek is in the context of him berating Mala, and this chastisement continues until she leaves him in Chapter One of Part Two. Given that neither Vladek nor Mala show signs of being content with each other, we might wonder why the pair remain together as long as they do. This raises the concept of survivor companionship and connection. We learn that Mala is also a Holocaust survivor whose family was devastated by the war. Presumably, this was what once afforded the couple their connection. It would seem, however, that their profound displacement and ongoing sadness as a result of the war is at odds with their ability to be happy with each other – perhaps the shadows of their respective survival stories are too great for them to live happily ever after. They each have demons from the war to grapple with.

Anja Spiegelman (nee Zylberberg)

Key quotes

'I have a good family ... a fine son ... I should be happy ... But I don't care. *I just don't want to live.*' (p.33, frames 3 and 4)

'... Artie ... you ... still ... love ... me ... don't you?' (p.105, frame 4)

'Let me alone! I don't want to live!' (p.124, frame 6)

'Just seeing you again gives me strength.' (p.216, frame 7)

Anja is Vladek's wife and Artie's mother. Born into a wealthy Jewish Polish family, Anja has grown up privileged and in want of very little until the war begins. Anja is described as relatively unattractive, unlike the beautiful women that Vladek has associated with until he meets her – so much so that Vladek is accused of marrying Anja for her money. Nevertheless, the two marry, and Vladek inherits part of the Zylberberg hosiery business.

Anja is a quiet and emotional individual who struggles throughout most of the novel to find happiness. Signs of Anja's depression are seen early in Vladek's relationship with her: Vladek looks through Anja's closet when he first visits her family and finds pills that a friend later tells him are for Anja's being 'skinny and nervous' (p.21, frame 6). She suffers severe post-natal depression after she gives birth to the couple's first son, Richieu, and she often talks of ending her life, particularly when the couple are incarcerated in Auschwitz. Unlike Vladek, Anja looks Jewish and struggles to hide her identity when the couple flee or attempt to hide. Once the war is over, the two are reunited, with Vladek saying, 'We were both very happy and lived happy, happy ever after' (p.296, frame 4) – but we know that this is not entirely true, given Anja's suicide twenty-three years later.

Anja only features in Vladek's retellings of his life, and we learn of her suicide very early on in the novel. The Anja that we witness during the war and the lead up to it is, for this reason, fractured. Anja's dialogue is scant and her presence as a character minimal. Artie is forced to rely on his father's depiction of her, and the effect of this is a mere shadow of a person in the wartime stories.

One reason why we do not learn a great deal about Anja is because Vladek burns all of her diaries and papers, preventing Artie from reading them and finding out about the mother he never properly knew. It is with great anger and frustration that Artie proclaims his father to be a 'murderer' (p.161, frame 4) because his mother's memories have been destroyed by Vladek's thoughtlessness – despite Anja's desire for her son to 'be interested by' (p.161, frame 3) her life when he grows up. This absence is certainly felt by the reader, and Artie reflects on this too, acknowledging that without her 'sensitive' story his novel lacks 'balance' (p.134, frame 4).

Yet by including his autobiographical comix, 'Prisoner on the Hell Planet', Artie shows us the reasons for his disconnection from his mother, and the profound effect her death has had on his psyche. It is difficult to ignore the Holocaust imagery in the comix, seen in Artie's dress – that of a prison inmate, similar to the uniform worn by those in Auschwitz – and in the Hitler-esque representation of the doctor. By depicting himself as a prisoner, we see that the mental effect that Anja's suicide had on Artie was imprisoning. In doing this, Spiegelman communicates his own holocaust story – his own turmoil and inability to escape.

Richieu Spiegelman

Key quotes

'I didn't think about him much when I was growing up ... He was mainly a large, blurry photograph hanging in my parents' bedroom.' (p.175, frame 4)

'But at least we could've made *him* go deal with Vladek. ... It's *spooky*, having sibling rivalry with a snapshot!' (p.175, frame 8)

Richieu grows to be 'only five or six' (p.175, frame 2) before becoming a victim of the war. It is interesting to note that like Anja, Richieu has very little dialogue in the novel, reminding us of his absolute silence, his death. It is clear that Richieu's presence remains in Vladek's life, as Artie observes. Richieu is often included in frames where Vladek is talking to members of his family, and when Vladek is frightened by the bodies of his Jewish trading partners hanging outside, Richieu is drawn playing with a doll at his feet. Vladek remembers his dead son fondly, referring to him as a 'happy, beautiful boy' (p.111, frame 9), and at the novel's conclusion he tells Artie, 'I'm *tired* from talking, Richieu' – ending, rather profoundly, on a point of sheer loss and fatigued delusion (p.296, frame 6).

Artie's discussion of his brother is neither detached nor affectionate. Artie seems very aware that Richieu's death is a loss that does not affect him personally, but he is scornful of the son that Richieu could have been. Presumably, this is not because Artie has any solid reason to dislike the brother he never met, but rather, this disdain for Richieu is because of Artie's parents' treatment of Artie himself. He refers to Richieu pleasing his parents in ways that Artie clearly has not – for example, should he have survived the Holocaust, Richieu might have 'become a doctor, and married a wealthy Jewish girl' (p.175, frame 7). These are things that Vladek and Anja wanted for Artie (they urged Art to become a dentist), which he resisted. Alternatively, Artie's disdain for Richieu could be due to – again – the survivor guilt that plagues him throughout the process of writing the novel.

Mala Spiegelman

Key quotes

'*All* our friends went through the camps. *Nobody* is like him!' (p.133, frame 6)

'I feel like I'm in prison! I feel like I'm going to *burst*!' (p.132, frame 8)

'It's an important book. People who don't usually read such stories will be interested.' (p.135, frame 3)

Mala is the incredibly patient but aggrieved second wife of Vladek. She features throughout the later chronology, as she lives with Vladek in Rego Park and Florida, and is often a significant presence during the interviews that Artie conducts with his father. Artie tells us that Vladek and Mala do not 'get along' (p.13, frame 6), and this is made clear as Vladek continually refers to Mala as a burden, lamenting his many woes, from her plain cooking to her apparent theft of his money when she leaves him.

It is unclear whether Vladek's complaints are legitimate – and it is surprising that Mala remains in a relationship with a man who so loudly and flagrantly complains about her – but there is a gentle voice of reason in Mala that cannot be ignored. She is clearly pained in many of her dealings with Vladek, and the reader, along with Artie, does not blame her for leaving Vladek in Chapter One of Part Two. Mala, too, has her own story: from the snippets of conversations that Artie has with her, we learn that she also lost most of her family in Auschwitz.

The reader cannot help but feel sympathy for the woman who puts up with Vladek's neuroses, despite how negative he is towards her, when she also has trauma from the war to grapple with. By giving us parts of Mala's history, Spiegelman shows that all survivors have their own stories of horror and loss; there are literally hundreds of thousands of individual stories to be told.

Françoise Mouly

Key quotes

'*Nobody's* normal.' (p.174, frame 8).

'How can you, of all people, be such a racist! You talk about blacks the way the Nazis talked about the Jews!' (p.259, frame 5).

Françoise is Artie's wife, and features prominently throughout the novel in the later chronology, while Artie visits his father to interview him. Françoise is Artie's sounding board and support over the difficulties that Vladek presents in Artie's life. She is a reasonable and sensitive woman who converted to Judaism for Artie's father, and wants Artie to draw her as a mouse too. Françoise becomes angry when Vladek chastises her for giving an African American hitchhiker (the 'shvartser', represented as a black dog) a lift, flabbergasted that he can be so racist when he was the victim of profound racism and persecution during the war.

It is through Françoise's presence in the novel that we are given access to many of Artie's reflections, as he often discusses his ideas, and reflects on the process of completing the novel, with her. Françoise also assists Artie in making sense of his father. Her character provides exposition at times, seen in dialogue such as 'maybe Auschwitz made him like that' (p.182, frame 6), allowing us to follow as the couple make sense of Vladek for themselves. Although Françoise describes Vladek as 'claustrophic' (p.182, frame 5), she has a respectful and supportive attitude towards him. Not only did Françoise convert to Judaism before she and Artie married in order to please Vladek, but in the Catskills she helps him with his banking papers and offers to stay with him longer to assist him, indicating the respect that she has for him.

THEMES, IDEAS & VALUES

Tragedy and loss

Key quotes

'We watched until they disappeared from our eyes ...' (p.110, frame 3)

'I'm telling you, it was a tragedy among tragedies.' (p.111, frame 9)

'He was a millionaire, but even this didn't save him his life.' (p.117, frame 6)

'*All* what is left, it's the photos.' (p.275, frame 7)

The notion of tragedy and loss in this novel is obvious: it is a war story. Vladek tells of profound loss, with only his brother, Pinek, surviving the war. While to many readers the scale of this loss may seem unimaginable, it is something that is very real to all survivors of the war. Entire families were wiped out in Hitler's Final Solution (a plan to exterminate all Jewish people in Nazi-occupied Europe).

In *Maus*, some are shown to be utterly devastated and overwhelmed by their grief. Throughout the novel there are instances where Anja is so grief-stricken that she says she wants to die, and we know that ultimately she does not survive her depression. Others, such as Vladek, are shown to have a more objective way of looking at the tragedies that surround them. Rather than being overcome with his grief and loss, Vladek observes the catastrophes around him and makes sure that he supports Anja, doing everything in his power to ensure that he too does not fall victim to tragedy.

The Holocaust is extremely difficult to come to terms with because of how widespread and devastating it was. It can be jarring to view this story unfolding in a comic book because the form may seem to detract from the gravity of the Holocaust. Because of this, *Maus* can unsettle the reader, but in doing so, it argues that no form of re-creating or retelling the events of the Holocaust will be easy to comprehend.

War and suffering

Key quotes

'At that time it *wasn't* anymore families. It was everybody to take care for *himself!*' (p.116, frame 5)

'To die, it's *easy* ... But you have to *struggle* for life! Until the last moment we must struggle together!' (p.124, frames 7–9)

'How amazing it is that a human being reacts the same like this neighbor's dog.' (p.242, frame 6)

Maus shows the lengths that people go to in order to survive. Vladek and his family are betrayed again and again by people simply wanting to protect themselves in the face of death during a bitter and gruesome war. Spiegelman divulges to us how humanity is capable of turning against itself during trying times – but he does so in a way that discourages us from criticising those who did wrong to others (even the Nazis). We learn that no-one is safe from the trials of war and the suffering inflicted by it – even those who betray Vladek for some small degree of safety.

Key point

Perhaps it is here where we see that we should ultimately admire Vladek, for he wishes no particular harm on anyone, despite what he has gone through. For a man who endured much suffering and torture and who came very close to death, Vladek is never bitter about his experiences. He is not generally represented as hating anyone or vowing revenge on those who persecuted him.

It is clear, though, that the hardship and suffering that Vladek has endured is something that is not understood by anyone other than him, and that perhaps he may not entirely understand himself, owing to the fact that his existence appears fractured and broken in his later life. Even his son, Artie, can only attempt to piece together Vladek's sense of grief and loss, and it is in this process of trying to mediate his father's story that Artie feels inadequate, and unable to make sense of how he feels about the war himself. Suffering certainly has had lasting effects on Vladek, and these effects make him a very difficult man to deal with. Because of what he has endured, we do not want to dislike Vladek, but it is understandable to dislike a man who is a bigot, racist and generally intolerable.

Here the theme of war and suffering becomes particularly complex: the product of this war and suffering, rather than evoking regret and sympathy in the reader, is negative and frustrating. Great horror and suffering is chronicled throughout the pages, but the examples of Vladek's trying personality peppered throughout the narrative at times appear to be given more weight than the events of the war. Speigelman thus suggests that the harmful effects of war do not end with the conclusion of a war, but in fact become integral aspects of the person who experienced them.

Death

Key quotes

'...You *murdered* me, Mommy, and you left me here to take the rap!' (p.105, frame 9)

'It's as if life equals winning, so death equals losing.' (p.205, frame 2)

Death is all around during war, and it is certainly a frequent presence in *Maus*. However, the way in which death is often presented in the novel demonstrates the mentality that those involved had to exercise in order to get on with life during this time. Because death was so prevalent, many people adopted a rather objective and pragmatic view of life and death. In this way, death is often presented in a very offhand or straightforward manner: a story will be told of someone's death and then the story will progress straight away, moving on to another (at times, minor) point of the narrative. We see this in Vladek's narration – he is quite matter-of-fact about the losses that occurred being plot points in his story, and he presents such events candidly, not holding back on detail.

Key point

Throughout the novel, the notion of the frailty of human life is explored. During the wartime narrative, we see the Germans' ability to terminate human life in split-second decisions or simply on a whim. In this, Spiegelman shows us not only the brutality of this war, but also the extent of meaningless loss that occurred.

Maus brings up prevailing questions of 'why' and 'how' that surfaced after the war, questions that will probably continue to be asked for many years to come. When we are presented with such cruel and vicious people, wiping out so many lives in such determined and horrific ways, we naturally question how this could have occurred on so large a scale. We feel Vladek's fear when he has various brushes with death, because we see how real the threat of death is to all Jewish people during the war.

Guilt

Key quotes

'Every word is like an unnecessary stain on silence and nothingness.' (p.205, frame 6)

'I guess it's *some* kind of guilt about having had an easier life than they did.' (p.176, frame 3)

'Maybe EVERYONE has to feel guilty. EVERYONE! FOREVER!' (p.202, frame 4)

In presenting one of the greatest and most devastating human tragedies of the twentieth century (the Jewish Holocaust), *Maus* asks us to grapple with how we feel about loss on such a scale. This is brought out by the fact that Artie – a child of the Holocaust generation – is unable to make sense of his guilt. Artie's feeling of inadequacy is no doubt rooted in a profound sense of guilt, to which he openly admits, and he represents all of the niggling and frustrating traits of Vladek to enable us to understand his struggle with the mix of guilt and frustration that he feels towards his father. In Chapter One of Part Two, Artie freely admits the weight of the guilt he feels to Françoise, and then he acknowledges it to the reporters and his psychiatrist at the beginning of the next chapter. It is admissions such as these that make *Maus* the autobiographical account that it is – as much as it is a retelling of a man's (Vladek's) experiences of the war, it is also an account of a man's (Art Spiegelman's) process of making sense of his guilt.

Holocaust survivor and writer Elie Wiesel has said, 'For the dead and the living, we must bear witness,' suggesting that witnesses of the Holocaust are not just those who were alive during it. Wiesel argues that bearing witness to the tragedy means never forgetting the tragedy for both the dead and the living, in the hope that ongoing discourse about it will honour those who perished. He suggests that we are all witnesses to the Holocaust, as we all continue to witness and feel its aftermath. With this, we are also invited to assess our own sense of guilt. This is not to say that any of us should feel responsible for the tragedy that occurred. It does call to mind, though, the very notion of being human: guilt and regret are universal human reactions to tragedies such as these, and *Maus* encourages us to feel these things in the hope that there will never be a repeat of such genocide.

Faith and luck

Key quotes

'You will come out of this place – *free!* On the day of Parshas Truma.' (p.59, frame 3)

'I started to believe. I tell you, he put another life in me.' (p.188, frame 8)

'But here God didn't come. We were all on our own.' (p.189, frame 9)

'I know there was a lot of LUCK involved, but he WAS amazingly present-minded and resourceful …' (p.205, frame 1)

'… and the Jews lived always with hope.' (p.233, frame 4)

Vladek constantly thinks ahead and is very resourceful. We see these traits continue in his later life as an old man (his extreme frugality is one of the characteristics that make him difficult to like). However, we are also invited to consider what role luck played in Vladek's experiences during the war. He has several brushes with death, and is often saved by quick thinking and on-the-spot plans that could have gone horribly wrong. With the notion of luck, we should consider the senseless nature of the loss of life that occurred during the war. With so little rhyme or reason to the killing, those who survived were clearly very fortunate, and they experienced luck against the odds. Only a very small proportion of Jews who entered Auschwitz made it out alive, with most – if not all – of the survivors being extremely close to death and so malnourished and overworked that they experienced long-term health problems for years after the war, both physically and psychologically.

For a devout Jewish man, Vladek does not talk much about how prayer or religious reflection assisted him in his survival. It is clear that many Jews practised their faith while in the death camps, but it would have been done in secret to escape the attention of German guards. The significance of Parshas Truma in Vladek's life invites us to consider fate, and whether or not there was indeed a greater force that contributed to Vladek's survival. Of course, this will never be answered; but the coincidences around Parshas Truma no doubt served Vladek in providing him with the impetus to carry on and not give up.

Memories

Key quotes

'Such things it's good to know exactly how was it – just in case …' (p.112, frame 6)

'Who knows … it *was* German prisoners also … Or they sent him to the gas, I don't remember …' (p.210, frames 4–5)

'No. I remember only *marching*, not any orchestras…' (p.214, frame 3)

'More I don't need to tell you. We were both very happy and lived happy, happy ever after.' (p.296, frame 4)

There is a prevailing idea throughout *Maus* about remembering, about never forgetting the horrors that were committed during the war. The novel asks us to share in Vladek's memories and the process with which Artie extracts his father's story. In this way, we become part of the memory, and we too become custodians of Vladek's story.

Maus shows us the problems that occur when human memory is relied upon. Because there is little surviving documentation of events in the concentration camps, we have to rely on the retellings of the few survivors. In *Maus*, we are relying on the account of an elderly survivor who is seen to struggle with detail as his story is divulged. The result is, at times, fractured – segments appear to finish abruptly, or details seem mismatched. On many occasions Artie prompts his father and pushes him for elaboration or further detail, and he also asks him to set things out chronologically.

Through this, we understand that Vladek's account is clearly retrospective, and it is important to note this, as retrospectives assume that their teller has had some ability to assess the events since they occurred. This means that they will have reflected on their feelings and memories, and their accounts will be coloured by the way that they look back on the events in question. For example, we see two very different Vladeks throughout the novel: Vladek, the protagonist in the wartime narrative; and Vladek, the father in the present-day narrative. Through this, we see that the person Vladek believes he was is quite different from the Vladek that Artie sees.

Nevertheless, Vladek's recollections are frequently vivid and detailed; they may be occasionally unreliable, but they also have the force and conviction of truth and experience.

Reconstructing and making sense of tragedy

Key quotes

'Just thinking about my book ... it's so *presumptuous* of me.' (p.174, frame 5)

'Reality is too *complex* for comics... so much has to be left out or distorted.' (p.176, frame 6)

'You – you *murderer*! How the hell could you do such a thing!!' (p.161, frame 4)

'... I can't even make any sense out of my relationship with my father ... How am I supposed to make any sense out of *Auschwitz*? ... Of the *Holocaust*?' (p.174, frame 6)

'It's almost impossible to believe Auschwitz ever happened.' (p.234, frame 6)

Artie experiences great difficulty in reconstructing his father's history, and this is made clear by his numerous reflections on the process. He wants to honour the suffering and plight of the Jews who experienced the Holocaust, but he constantly questions his ability to do so faithfully. He is shown to doubt himself and feel uncertain about his capacity to convey the story. As a way of presenting this truth, Spiegelman gives a 'warts and all' representation of himself, as well as of Vladek. When Artie visits his psychiatrist, Pavel, he discusses the problems he is having in reconstructing his father's story. It is very important to Artie to present reality, and he admits that he does this partly by depicting the anger and frustration that he feels towards his father – Artie is hence represented as irritable and exasperated for much of the time he is dealing with his father.

Key point

Artie is unable to visualise aspects of Vladek's story; in this way, Spiegelman suggests the impossibility of fully understanding or conceptualising what the Jews experienced in the Holocaust.

DIFFERENT INTERPRETATIONS

Different interpretations arise from different responses to a text. Over time, a text will give rise to a wide range of responses from its readers, who may come from various social or cultural groups and live in very different places and historical periods. Responses by critics and reviewers can be published in newspapers, journals and books, both online and in print. They can also be expressed in discussions among readers in the media, classrooms, book groups and so on.

While there is no single correct reading or interpretation of a text, it is important to understand that an interpretation is more than a personal opinion – it is the justification of a point of view on the text. To present an interpretation of a text based on your point of view, you must use a logical argument and support it with relevant evidence from the text.

The critics' viewpoints

In *MetaMaus*, Art Spiegelman says that 'rejections [for *Maus*] came from almost every reputable publisher', with editors apparently unable to make sense of a Holocaust story in comic-book form. Criticisms in some of these rejection letters were particularly strong: the editors felt unable to support so raw and serious an issue as the Holocaust being represented through the animal metaphor. Some, however, rejected *Maus* with regret, knowing that what they were refusing would some day be great; rejections from these publishers identified that the content and style did not accord with their particular viewpoint. Needless to say, once Spiegelman did manage to secure a publishing company (Pantheon) to take his project on, the graphic novel soared to successes that Spiegelman never thought possible. In *MetaMaus* again, Spiegelman tells his interviewer that he only thought his work 'would be appreciated posthumously' (p.79).

There is no paucity of admirers of Art Spiegelman today. He is highly regarded in the New York art scene, with 'most observers [agreeing] that no single person has done more to achieve [the] cultural repositioning of the comics medium' (Witek 2007, p.xi). Joseph Witek, writing in *Art Spiegelman: Conversations*, lauds Spiegelman as an experimenter whose will to test the boundaries of literature and the comix medium provides us, in *Maus*, with a 'defining moment in the emergence of comics as a serious art form' (Witek 2007, p.xi). In this way, Witek sees Spiegelman's work as being of great importance in the industry, as it epitomises the comic book in form and purpose: Witek argues that the 'unprecedented popularity' and true triumph of *Maus* is that it 'brought comics to the attention of a wide and varied readership' (Witek 2007, p.xiii). Critics are particularly complimentary of *Maus*' triple-level narrative structure, and the way in which it chronicles the difficulties one experiences when trying to chart horrific experiences second-hand.

Many critics also laud *Maus* as a triumph in storytelling, in that rather than providing a first-hand account of Vladek's experiences of the war (giving us Vladek as the protagonist in his wartime narrative), Spiegelman adds a profound level to his novel by showing us the process that he – as artist and author – undertook in creating his father's story. In his essay 'Necessary Stains: Art Spiegelman's *Maus* and the Bleeding of History', Michael G. Levine refers to this phenomenon as an example of 'postmemory', where the reader is given the story of the survivor's child 'whose life [has been] dominated by memories that preceded [their] birth' (Levine 2006, p.17). It is in divulging his father's story through this 'postmemory' function, Levine suggests, that Spiegelman defines 'an important turning point in the history of the Holocaust testimony' (Levine 2006, p.16), one that moves away from the normal and more traditional methods of retelling the horrific events of war.

Two interpretations

The following discussion shows how two contrasting interpretations of *The Complete Maus* can be supported with textual evidence. Note that the two provide very different interpretations of character, but both are supported with specific examples of dialogue, behaviour or events.

Interpretation 1: *Maus* offers the reader no uplifting messages.

Because the subject matter of *Maus* is confronting, the novel will naturally, at times, be challenging to read. Partly this is because the horrors of the highly documented Jewish Holocaust are known by most – the wartime narrative aspect of the novel is not new, and the reader is capable of anticipating what is to come. The fact that we have the Holocaust survivor's story being told – in part – by this survivor himself presents us with, perhaps, the only positive message of the novel: he survived. It can be said that all else we see in the text is rather bleak and dismal.

Maus ends with a sad and somewhat haunting image: the tombstone of Vladek and Anja Spiegelman – one of the few frames in the novel without borders, signifying its everlasting message. It is a fairly dark and depressing aspect for a graphic novel to end on. We are reminded of Anja's suicide in that the date of her death is some years before Vladek's, and this is jarring, as only a few frames before we have Vladek's somewhat insincere comment about living 'happy, happy ever after' (p.296, frame 4) with Anja.

A significant part of the sadness of this novel is that we see how profoundly affected by the subject its author is. The honesty with which Art Spiegelman recounts the process of extracting the story from his father provides us with a sense of how fractured his relationship with Vladek is. There is much candour in the sheer struggle that Artie experiences with a father who is difficult and neurotic, apparently unaware of the burden he and his demons pose on the lives of those around him. The novel's dismal ending is bookended by a fairly austere opening, with the prologue capturing the tenor of Spiegelman's childhood relationship with his father – a fractured and cold one that does not seem to change throughout the course of the novel. The lack of comfort and support that Vladek gives his son certainly sets a sad tone for the pair's relationship, and it is just one way Spiegelman shows his reader that he has, throughout his life, been living in the shadow of his parents' survival story.

Spiegelman has said it was important that he did not sentimentalise or create a heroic figure in Vladek, and he has indeed created a 'warts-and-all' relationship in which both Vladek and Artie can appear 'really unpleasant' (Spiegelman 2011, p.33). This shows us that, although we can consider *Maus* an autobiography about a man connecting with his father and learning of his past, it is not necessarily a triumphant one. At no point in the novel is Artie contented or fulfilled by the process. Rather, he finds writing *Maus* an incredibly difficult and trying undertaking, one that is buttressed by his depression and therapy (both seen in Chapter Two of Part Two). Spiegelman was immensely affected by his parents' demons. Perhaps the process of telling their story was actually not cathartic for him, as the distress he felt through the process is so honestly and vividly depicted.

The other profoundly bleak aspect of the novel is not so much in Vladek's horrible and gruelling wartime narrative, but in the aftermath of it. In providing a 'warts-and-all' account of his father, Spiegelman demonstrates that the horrors of the war shaped the person that Vladek grew into after he survived it. With a life reduced to 'not even a snapshot' (p.276, frame 7), the ghosts of Vladek's past frame him as an everlasting survivor: a man who 'ever since Hitler' does not like to throw out 'even a crumb' (p.238, frame 7); a man who 'in some ways ... didn't survive' (p.250, frame 2). The result is a fractured individual who is difficult to deal with – childish at times and possessing a petulant temperament. It can be very difficult to like Vladek. This particularly comes to the fore when, in Chapter Three of Part Two, Vladek is bigoted and racist in his chastisement of Françoise for giving an African American man (represented as a black dog) a lift. This presents Vladek as a man who does not seem to care about the unjust treatment of different social groups and races, a quality which is jarring and difficult to accept, given what he has gone through in his own life. This shows us that he is not necessarily a nice person, and it provides a rather negative representation of his postwar personality, rather than a positive, uplifting message about survival.

Interpretation 2: In *Maus* we see that the experience of war continues to influence the lives of survivors and their families.

We know that people who experience war are often haunted by it for many years afterwards. The incredible physical trauma experienced by European Jews in the Holocaust is well documented, but the psychological trauma is less so, due to the difficulty of reaching definite conclusions and ascertaining statistics about problems of the mind. There are a number of factors that would contribute to the psychological problems of Holocaust survivors, including survivor guilt, the imprint of death on the mind of the individual and a search for meaning after the war. These factors prevail in the survivor's mind; while the events of the war and the physical trauma may have ended, the mind can continue to be traumatised by what happened, and will attempt to make sense of this long after.

There are many examples throughout *Maus* that demonstrate to us that the characters, both survivors and not, have been, and will continue to be, affected by the events of World War II. When Artie begins interviewing his father, the war has been over for almost thirty years, but Vladek is very obviously still affected by it. This is seen in his personality and in his relationships with others. Vladek's demeanour is difficult: he is incredibly critical of the people around him, and he is excessively needy and hypocritical; he hoards things unnecessarily and is stingy with his money. We get the sense that Vladek, in keeping menus from cruises, stationery from hotels and pitchers from the hospital, has set about filling his life with meaningless possessions simply to have them and be in control of them.

This is somewhat understandable when we remember that during the war, Jews were robbed of their possessions, and survivors of the concentration camps came out with nothing other than the clothes they wore. Vladek alludes to the lasting effects the war has on him when he says, 'I cannot forget it ... ever since Hitler I don't like to throw out even a crumb' (p.238, frame 7). In this, we have an admission that the war haunts him and affects how he lives.

From the way in which Vladek interacts with the people around him, we understand that he is difficult to get along with (quite different from the man he describes in his wartime narrative). Spiegelman shows us this through his depiction of Artie, Mala and Françoise as they struggle to communicate with Vladek and are frustrated by his various neuroses. Vladek does not have a single nice thing to say about Mala throughout the novel, and his interactions with Artie are unpredictable, at best. It is clear that Vladek has not handled his demons after the war well. Mala tells us that she too 'went through the camps' and that 'nobody is like him', despite going through similar traumas (p.133).

Another 'survivor's tale' in this novel is Artie's. A transfer of trauma has occurred from Vladek and Anja to Artie. In this way, the experiences of war can be said to be heritable (able to be passed on from parent to child), and the Holocaust is something that Artie has clearly grappled with for most of his life. From the events of the prologue and Artie's problems with Vladek throughout the course of the novel, we see that his parents have passed their trauma on to him and not assisted him in coping with it. Artie tells us early on that his mother committed suicide, and we know from 'Prisoner on the Hell Planet' that Artie spent time in a mental hospital. We know, also, that Artie's psychological treatment is ongoing, with his visit to his psychiatrist, Pavel, represented in Chapter Two of Part Two. These things all show that Artie's trauma is real and that it is definitely related to his parents' experiences of the Holocaust. While we do not know the exact reasons for Artie beginning to write the novel, it is clear that throughout the process of interviewing Vladek and creating the text, a certain level of catharsis occurs. We see this in Artie's ongoing reflections, particularly in Part Two.

In these ways, we see that the experiences of the war are felt not just by those who lived through war but by those close to them, and that they are not confined by time or place.

QUESTIONS & ANSWERS

This section focuses on your own analytical writing on the text, and gives you strategies for producing high-quality responses in your coursework and exam essays.

Essay writing – an overview

An essay on a literary work is a formal and serious piece of writing that presents your point of view on the text, usually in response to a given topic. Your 'point of view' in an essay is your interpretation of the meaning of the text's language, structure, characters, situations and events, supported by detailed analysis of textual evidence.

Analyse – don't summarise

In your essays it is important to avoid simply summarising what happens in a text.

- A **summary** is a description or paraphrase (retelling in different words) of the characters and events. For example: 'Macbeth has a horrifying vision of a dagger dripping with blood before he goes to murder King Duncan.'
- An **analysis** is an explanation of the real meaning or significance that lies 'beneath' the text's words (and images, for a film). For example: 'Macbeth's vision of a bloody dagger shows how deeply uneasy he is about the violent act he is contemplating – as well as his sense that supernatural forces are impelling him to act.'

A limited amount of summary is sometimes necessary to let your reader know which part of the text you wish to discuss. However, always keep this to a minimum and follow it immediately with your analysis of what this part of the text is really telling us.

Plan your essay

Carefully plan your essay so that you have a clear idea of what you are going to say. The plan ensures that your ideas flow logically, that your argument remains consistent and that you stay on the topic. An essay plan should be a list of **brief dot points** – no more than half a page.

- Include your central argument or main contention – a concise statement (usually in a single sentence) of your overall response to the topic. See 'Analysing a sample topic' for guidelines on how to formulate a main contention.
- Write three or four dot points for each paragraph indicating the main idea and evidence/examples from the text. Note that in your essay you will need to *expand* on these points and *analyse* the evidence.

Structure your essay

An essay is a complete, self-contained piece of writing. It has a clear beginning (the introduction), middle (several body paragraphs) and end (the last paragraph or conclusion). It must also have a central argument that runs throughout, linking each paragraph to form a coherent whole.

See examples of introductions and conclusions in the 'Analysing a sample topic' and 'Sample answer' sections.

The introduction establishes your overall response to the topic. It includes your main contention and outlines the main evidence you will refer to in the course of the essay. Write your introduction after you have done a plan and before you write the rest of the essay.

The body paragraphs argue your case – they present evidence from the text and explain how this evidence supports your argument. Each body paragraph needs:

- a strong **topic sentence** (usually the first sentence) that states the main point being made in the paragraph
- **evidence** from the text, including some brief quotations

- **analysis** of the textual evidence, explaining its significance, and **explanation** of how it supports your argument
- **links back to the topic** in one or more statements, usually towards the end of the paragraph.

Connect the body paragraphs so that your discussion flows smoothly. Use some linking words and phrases such as 'similarly' and 'on the other hand', though don't start every paragraph like this. Another strategy is to use a significant word from the last sentence of one paragraph in the first sentence of the next.

Use key terms from the topic – or synonyms for them – throughout, so the relevance of your discussion to the topic is always clear.

The conclusion ties everything together and finishes the essay. It includes strong statements that emphasise your central argument and provide a clear response to the topic.

Avoid simply restating the points made earlier in the essay – this will end on a very flat note and imply that you have run out of ideas and vocabulary. The conclusion is meant to be a logical extension of what you have written, not just a repetition or summary of it. Writing an effective conclusion can be a challenge. Try using these tips:

- Start by linking back to the final sentence of the second-last paragraph – this helps your writing to 'flow', rather than leaping back to your main contention straight away.
- Use synonyms and expressions with equivalent meanings to vary your vocabulary. This allows you to reinforce your line of argument without being repetitive.
- When planning your essay, think of one or two broad statements or observations about the text's wider meaning. These should be related to the topic and your overall argument. Keep them for the conclusion, since they will give you something 'new' to say but still follow logically from your discussion. The introduction will be focused on the topic, but the conclusion can present a wider view of the text.

Essay topics

1. '*Maus* shows that surviving is sometimes worse than dying.' Discuss.
2. People do incredible things during war. How is this shown in Art Spiegelman's *Maus*?
3. How does *Maus* invite the reader to see the flaws as well as the strengths of its main characters?
4. 'Through *Maus*, Art Spiegelman shows us that the demons of the Holocaust will haunt us forever.' Discuss.
5. "Every word is like an unnecessary stain on silence and nothingness." 'It is in the "silences" of *Maus* that the most poignant messages are delivered.' To what extent to you agree?
6. How does Spiegelman invite the reader to question the validity of memory and perception?
7. 'The real "survivor's tale" is Artie's.' Do you agree?
8. How does Spiegelman use visual cues in *Maus* to alert us to the plight of his characters?
9. 'Despite the sadness depicted in *Maus*, it is ultimately a story of hope.' Discuss.
10. How does Spiegelman show us that Vladek is not the only Holocaust survivor?
11. '*Maus* would not be so powerful if it were a conventional novel.' Discuss.

Vocabulary for writing on *Maus*

Autobiography: an account of the events that make up one's own life. It is written by one person about themselves.

Biography: an account of the events that make up a person's life – their stories and history. It is written by one person about another.

Communism: a political philosophy that aims to abolish the class system in society, and advocates for collective ownership of businesses and enterprises.

Discourse: extended written or spoken communication about a topic or issue. Discourse is interactive, involving more than one party.

First-person narration: a form of storytelling presented from the point of view of the person experiencing the story, usually conveying events as they unfold.

Frames: a series of still pictures that contribute to a comic strip or collection of strips.

Genocide: the systematic killing of a racial or cultural group.

Graphic novel: a novel told in the form of frames and strips of drawings; a long comic strip that tells an extended story.

Heritable: something that is capable of being inherited or passed down through generations.

Holocaust: an act of mass destruction and loss of life. This term is most often associated with the Jewish Holocaust, the mass murder of Jews under the German Nazi regime from 1941 until 1945.

Inhumanity: a lack of compassion, understanding or mercy for others; a committing of acts of atrocious cruelty.

Interwar period: the period of time after World War I and before World War II; roughly 1920 to 1938.

Irony: incongruity (mismatch or difference) between what might be expected and what actually occurs.

Metaphor: a figure of speech in which an expression is used to refer to something that it does not literally denote in order to suggest a similarity. A visual metaphor is an image that is used to refer to something it does not literally denote in order to suggest a similarity.

Metafiction: fiction in which the author self-consciously alludes to potential artificiality in the work by alerting the reader to it, thereby parodying or departing from traditional conventions and narrative techniques in fiction.

Motif: a recurring idea or image that is used to convey meaning and alert the reader to deeper aspects of the work. Provides narrative cues that assist in the reader's understanding of themes, plot and characterisation.

Multimodal texts: texts that incorporate more than one mode of storytelling – combining, for example, visual and written language to convey the narrative.

Neurosis: a psychological state characterised by excessive anxiety, indecision, and a degree of social or interpersonal maladjustment.

Racism: the belief that members of one race are intrinsically superior to members of another race; discriminatory or abusive behaviour towards members of another race.

Reflection: a calm and considered recounting of one's thoughts, feelings and experiences; a weighing up of the way one feels about life and experiences.

Third-person narration: a form of storytelling presented from the point of view of the person viewing the action of the story.

Visual palimpsest: a visual layering of the past over the present, or the present over the past.

Wartime narrative: a story of one's time during the war.

Analysing a sample topic

How does Spiegelman show us that Vladek is not the only Holocaust survivor?

This essay topic invites you to consider the notion that the emotional aftermath of the Jewish Holocaust was something that affected not only survivors but also their children and those close to them. The assumption here is that Artie's suffering, while very different from his father's, is felt in a comparable way. Because *Maus* is a graphic novel, you should always attempt to discuss the visual aspect of the novel, as well as the written content, the text's structure and the various levels of narrative; these elements all contribute to the way that we understand the story and characters. Don't limit your discussion only to Vladek and Artie: this topic encourages you to examine the idea that Vladek's story is an example of many people's suffering.

The topic invites you to think about the following questions.

- Vladek is a long-suffering Holocaust survivor. How is it made clear to us that his suffering extends beyond the duration of the war?
- Is one of the reasons there are so many characters in this novel that this gives us some indication of the sheer number of people affected by the Holocaust?
- How do Vladek's experiences of the war adversely affect those around him?
- Examine the suffering that Artie experiences as a result of having parents who are survivors of the Holocaust. How are we made aware of his suffering?
- Consider the narrative levels that provide us with Spiegelman's autobiographical reflections, and the discourse that takes place between Artie and Vladek. In what ways does Artie suffer in the process of creating *Maus*?
- Consider Artie's awareness of his depression and the way that his parents' experiences may have affected him. How does this connect to the idea of survivor guilt?
- The novel is original in that it visually depicts the suffering of its characters. How is this suffering conveyed, and how does the novel's form enable us to see this clearly?

The following plan is just one way to tackle this essay topic.

Sample introduction

> There is no denying that, in the first instance, Art Spiegelman's *Maus* is Vladek Spiegelman's 'survivor's tale'. Vladek's gripping and tragic account of his experiences during World War II and the Jewish Holocaust show the reader that the human spirit can overcome great trials and suffering in the face of death. Through Art Spiegelman's inclusion of various narrative levels that reveal the process he undertook in procuring his father's story, the reader is also provided with an account of how the war affects

Vladek many years later. These narrative levels, along with visual cues, invite the reader to consider the notion that survival is not a single event, but rather is ongoing, and affects the lives of those close to the survivor too.

Body paragraph outline

Paragraph 1: There are people other than Vladek who suffer.

- Interpreting the topic in a literal sense, examine the scope of the Holocaust; it affected the lives of millions of people.
- Many characters and their personal stories are conveyed throughout the course of the novel. Anja's suffering was so profound that she could not endure it. Mala is also a Holocaust survivor, who also went through the camps.

Paragraph 2: Surviving is a phenomenon that is passed down from parent to child.

- Because Vladek's suffering endures throughout his life, this suffering is felt by his son, Artie.
- Vladek also makes Artie suffer from his cantankerous personality.
- Guilt is something that is felt by children of survivors. In Vladek's absence, Artie feels that he has to carry around his father's traumas in order to do justice to Vladek's suffering.

Paragraph 3: Through Artie's reflections of drawing the novel, we see how much he is affected by the Holocaust, even though he did not experience it directly.

- Artie reflects on the process of drawing the novel and wants to be true to his father's story.
- The autobiographical nature of the novel shows us that Spiegelman uses it as a way to survive and make sense of history himself.
- The visual depictions of Artie dealing with Vladek show us the frustration and exasperation Artie feels.
- Artie's visit to Pavel, in which he appears as a child, shows us that he feels dwarfed by his father's demons.

- Françoise's role in the novel is to provide Artie with a sounding board and a reasonable voice which assist him to decode and analyse his feelings about his father.

Sample conclusion

While *Maus* provides the reader with a compelling account of Vladek's trials and suffering throughout World War II, it is difficult to overlook the effect that his experiences have on others. Through the multi-tiered structure of the novel that allows us to see Artie's reflective process, we understand the weight of Vladek's sorrows on Artie's shoulders. This weight is manifested not only in his guilt for not having a firsthand understanding of his parents' suffering, but also in how difficult Vladek is to deal with. The older Vladek is not an easy man to like, but his neurotic behaviour is clearly a result of his traumatic wartime experiences. Spiegelman conveys the darkness that plagues not only the mind of the sufferer, but also the minds of those close to the traumatised individual.

SAMPLE ANSWER

'*Maus* would not be so powerful if it were a conventional novel.' Discuss.

With a chronology spanning decades, one powerful aspect of Art Spiegelman's compelling graphic novel, *Maus*, is its wartime narrative. Presented visually, it is a story of suffering and survival. The fact that the text is a graphic novel enables the author to communicate numerous narrative layers arising from his extraction of the wartime narrative from his father. It is the novel's visual representation of characters and their relationships with one another that delivers one of Spiegelman's most powerful messages: to survive the war is to engage in a lifelong struggle that haunts for years to come.

Providing us with a horrific story of war and persecution but offering some hope in the survival of some of its characters, *Maus* asks us to consider some very dark themes. The fact that genocide can occur on such a large scale is horrifying and shocking, but we are buoyed by Vladek's survival of the Holocaust, against the odds. Visually, Spiegelman creates a chaotic world that charts Vladek's experiences in the lead up to the war and then his time at Auschwitz. Through his drawings, Spiegelman conveys the darkness of the war and the horror felt by those who experienced it. One cannot look past the significance of the animals used to depict the German, Jewish and Polish races. Spiegelman uses cats, mice and pigs – representing predator, prey and bystander – to depict his characters but also to draw, ironically, on Adolf Hitler's metaphor: he once referred to the Jewish race as vermin that needed to be eradicated. Symbols are embedded in the novel to depict the rise of Nazism and the terror felt by people as the Nazi presence grew. The symbol of the Nazi swastika rising over the city of Brandenberg, dwarfing the town below it, alerts us to the fact that the Nazi rise was widely felt and feared. In addition, Spiegelman uses illustrations and diagrams to provide facts to his reader and to clarify details of his father's story.

Because the novel is graphic, Spiegelman is able to mingle different narrative levels more seamlessly; this makes for a powerful device for melding together the stories of Vladek and Artie. Laced throughout Vladek's wartime narrative is Spiegelman's story of extracting this narrative from his father. By providing us with a visual representation of both, Spiegelman affords his tale an honesty that could otherwise be lost without visual depiction. Interjections provide the reader with an understanding of how the extraction unfolds, and Artie's interactions with his father show us that it is a difficult process for Artie to uncover and write about his father's ordeal. Although subtle, the autobiographical level of the novel is made clearer and most poignant by its visual representation. This is seen at the beginning of 'Auschwitz (Time Flies)', where Artie speaks directly to the reader atop a mound of dead bodies with flies hovering around him. The bodies and flies appear to follow Artie as he walks the streets to his psychiatrist, and from this, the reader can glean that Artie's guilt haunts him wherever he goes. These are visual cues that provide profound messages to the reader, increasing the text's power.

By drawing characters and their interactions with one another, Spiegelman is able to convey a more vivid picture of their relationships. The reader witnesses the exasperation Artie feels in his dealings with his father, and can sense Vladek's frustrations in being a survivor and struggling to deal with life after the war and the Holocaust. Dialogue is complemented by characters' facial expressions and physical gestures. In 'Mouse Holes', Vladek is clearly upset with Artie, and this is shown not only by his dialogue but also, more particularly, by how Spiegelman represents Vladek visually: he is hunched over his work and peers over his spectacles, completing a menial task while not engaging with his son. The reader feels the tension by witnessing it visually. In contrast, most depictions of interactions between Artie and Françoise show a certain closeness between the two. When the couple leave their holiday to care for Vladek in 'Mauschwitz', their conversation is faithfully depicted frame by frame. This series of close-ups of the couple show the intimacy and understanding that they share, and we see through this visual depiction that Françoise is of great support to her husband.

By offering his 'survivor's tale' as a graphic novel, Art Spiegelman gives his reader more connection and engagement with the narrative levels used to tell his multi-layered story. As Artie acknowledges, 'Every word is like an unnecessary stain on silence and nothingness', and it is by presenting his story visually that Spiegelman allows his reader to silently contemplate and reflect on the horrors of the Holocaust and of the emotional aftermath that prevails.

REFERENCES & READING

Text

Spiegelman, Art 1996, *The Complete Maus,* Penguin Books, London.

Books and journal articles

Arnold, Andrew 2007, 'Comix Poets', in *World Literature Today,* vol. 81, no. 2, pp.12–13.

Elmwood, Victoria 2004, '"Happy, Happy Ever After": The Transformation of Trauma Between the Generations in Art Spiegelman's *Maus: A Survivor's Tale',* in *Biography: An Interdisciplinary Quarterly*, vol. 27, no. 4, pp.691–720.

Geis, Deborah 2003, *Considering Maus: Approaches to Art Spiegelman's "Survivor's Tale" of the Holocaust*, University of Alabama Press, Tuscaloosa.

Hutcheon, Linda 1999, 'Literature Meets History: Counter-Discoursive "Comix"', in *Anglia: Zeitschrift für Englische Philogie*, vol. 117, no. 1, pp.4–14.

McGlothlin, Erin 2003, 'No Time Like the Present: Narrative and Time in Art Spiegelman's *Maus*', in *NARRATIVE*, vol. 11, no. 2, pp.177–98.

Spiegelman, Art 2011, *MetaMaus*, Penguin Books, London.

Witek, Joseph 2007, *Art Spiegelman: Conversations*, University Press of Mississippi, Jackson.

Websites

Art Spiegelman, Steven Barclay Foundation, http://barclayagency.com/spiegelman.html

Douillard, Andy 2005, *Do the Wounds Ever Heal? PTSD and Holocaust Survivors*, http://www.history.ucsb.edu/faculty/marcuse/classes/33d/projects/survivors/SurvivorPTSD_Andy05z.htm

Further reading

Spiegelman, Art 2004, *In the Shadow of No Towers*, Pantheon Books, New York.

Spiegelman, Art 2013, *Co-Mix*, Drawn and Quarterly, Montreal.